THE 1844 DIARY
of
JOHN WILLIAM SNEYD
Muskets and Mining

by

Marion Aldis and Pam Inder

Title Page: Watercolour of John William Sneyd, aged about fourteen, c1836
Artist unknown

Published by

CHURNET VALLEY BOOKS

43 Bath Street
Leek
Staffordshire
01538 399033

© Marion Aldis and Pam Inder and Churnet Valley Books
1996

ISBN 1897949 22 7

Printed in Great Britain by the Ipswich Book Company, Suffolk

Contents

John Sneyd
b.1734
d.1809

— m 1762 — **Penelope Kynnersley (of Loxley Hall)**

Children:

- Mary Anne
  b.1766
  d.
  m
  John Holley
  of Norfolk
  daughter Penelope

- **William**
  b.1767
  d.1840
  m
  Jane Debank
  of Stafford

- Clement
  b.1773
  d.1854
  m
  1. Helen Swetenham
  of Chester
  2 sons & 2 daugt.
  2. Eliza Cotton

  and others

- Thomas
  b.1774

  Took the name
  Sneyd-Kynnersley

- and others

Children of Mary Anne / John Holley branch:

- **John**
  b.1798
  d.1873
  m
  Penelope Holley
  1822

- Ralph
  b.1799
  d.1829

- Thomas
  b.1800
  d.1883

- Rev. Henry
  b.1804
  d.1859

- Mary
  b.1807
  d 1886

Children of John & Penelope Holley:

- Wm. DeBank
  b.1797
  d.1825

- **John William**
  b. 1822
  d. 1904
  m
  Agnes Cotton
  1861

- Harriet
  b.1824
  d.1857
  m
  Robert
  Bamford
  1850

- Emily Jane
  b.1825
  d.1901

- Penelope Marianne
  b.1826
  m
  John Clerk
  Brodie
  1848

- Helen
  b.1828
  d.1844

- Ralph Debank
  b.1830
  d.1854

- Susanna
  b.1831
  d.1891
  m
  Charles Ingleby
  1860

- Dryden Henry
  b.1833
  d.1913

- Lionel
  b.1835
  d.1853

- Mary.
  b.1837.
  d.1854

- Frederick
  b.1839
  d.1864

- Richard Wettenhall
  b. 1841
  d. 1863

- Gustavus Alfred
  b.1844
  d.1926
  m
  Christabell Harris
  1882

Child of John William & Agnes Cotton:

- **Ralph de
  Tunstall**
  b.1862

Acknowledgments

We would like to express our deep gratitude to Martin Phillips, Keeper of the Special Collections at Keele University Library for all his help and support.

We also thank all the members of the Sneyd family who have helped us so generously with information and illustrative material and in particular Averil Scott-Moncrieff, Colin and Joyce Shenton, Dr John Sneyd and Roger Wykes Sneyd, without whose help this book could not have been produced.

We are also grateful to the following individuals and institutions who have, in various ways, furthered our research:-
Richard Amies from the Sygon Copper Mine, Beddgelert
Edward Ash
Christine Chester
Professor Trevor Ford
Colonel David German of the Staffordshire Yeomanry Collection
Margaret Griffith
Barbara McCarthy
Roy Paulson
Professor John Pick
Lindsey Porter
Cynthia Thomas
Stephen Walker
The staff of the British Library Hanley Library, the Departments of Education and English Local History at Leicester University, the National Newspaper Library and the Record Offices at Lichfield and Stafford.

October [10th Mo] 27 **Sunday** [301–65] **1844**

21 Sun aft Trin. Mg, Habak ii, Luke xiii:
Ev, Prov i, Phil i

My Father & I went as far as Ipstones in the gig & walked on to Foot in the morning & came back to Ipstones in the afternoon.

~~~ 28 **MONDAY** [302–64] ~~~
St Simon and St Jude

My Father & I ... to breakfast ... my Fathers went in ... I in my gig ... ral meeting at Stone ... Sandon miles in the chair ... of ... was afternoon ... & Lord ... vice president for the ensuing year ... dence & ... tea ... my Grandfather had a letter

~~~ 29 **TUESDAY** [303–63] ~~~

I went out shooting ... & killed 1 hare 3 Partridges 8 ... rabbits. My Fathers ... at home settling Mr Bakers accounts ...

from Sir Thomas Shepherd ... the entry ... that Uncle ... strating at Longtonmarsh ... ding his gun he supposed ... in the barrel burst his hands ... and injured both his hands very much ...

DAY [304–62] [10th Month] **October**

& I attended the Justice ... called at ... as the ... to ... in the ... then thence to ... jail in the night

[?–61]

called on ... a ... is ... he went on ... the mine ... in a.

Extracts from John William's original diary, actual size.
Reproduced by courtesy of Keele University Library

INTRODUCTION

John William Sneyd was the first child of the Rev John Sneyd and his wife Penelope. He was born on October 9th 1822. The Sneyds were a minor gentry family who had for generations been major land and estate owners in the County of Staffordshire and as such were held in much esteem locally.

Throughout the whole of the nineteenth century most members of the family kept diaries and many of these survive. Only one of John William's has so far been found, though it is almost certain that he kept one regularly as a young man. His 1844 diary, written when he was 22, shows a young man full of vigour, and gives a clear glimpse of his life and also into the way of life of most young men in his strata of society at that time.

As in most land-owning families of the late eighteenth and early nineteenth centuries, lack of available money was not seen as a hindrance to spending very large sums. Borrowing money against land was common practice and the Sneyds were no exception. A slip of paper in the front of John William's grandfather's diary for 1828 shows that he had borrowed by that date in excess of £33,000 from various people, ranging from several thousands from friends and relatives to £25 from a servant. Figures from the Central Statistical Office have been used to try to equate this to present day values. It is an imprecise conversion but gives some idea of the sums of money involved and approximate present day valuations will be put in brackets throughout the introduction. £33,000 would be over one and a half million today!

Many landowners acted as unofficial banks borrowing money and investing it and paying interest of between 3 and 4% to the person from whom it was borrowed. Difficulty often arose when the capital was required to be repaid. This was probably what was happening when John William writes of "Ball's" or "Kenton's" business. Gentry families lived by credit, running up huge bills with local shopkeepers, tailors, bootmakers and so on - often only paying off part of their debts at the end of the year.

John William's father, the Rev John Sneyd, was the second son of William Sneyd of Ashcombe Park. He did not expect to inherit the fine house which his father had built or the extensive estate, and like many younger sons he looked to the church to provide him with a living and some status in the community. He took Holy Orders in 1821. In an era when a good many marriages in that level of society were arranged and had far more to do with consolidating and enlarging estates than romance, John William's parents seem to have married for love. The Rev John records that they were childhood companions and cousins and they married soon after John had completed his degree at Brasenose College Oxford. Penelope brought a settlement of £5,000 (£250,000) to the marriage and with that, a church living, the gift of his mother, Jane Debank Sneyd and money inherited from his grandmother, Elizabeth Debank, the Rev John and his new wife had a more than comfortable start to married life. John took the curacy at Odstone in Leicestershire as a first position and he and Penelope were soon on visiting terms with all the notable families in the area. It was there that John William, or Jonkey as he was affectionately known, was born.

In April 1825 the family returned to Staffordshire and took up residence at Basford Hall on the Ashcombe estate. Their furniture and other goods were sent by canal arriving at Froghall wharf, and with his characteristic energy the Rev John set about 'improving' Basford Hall. John William's earliest memories of Basford must have been of endless years of alterations and building work making the house cold, damp and noisy. Not surprisingly, his mother, who, like most wives at that time, was having a child every year or two, spent as much time away from the place as she could. Her diary reveals long periods spent with family and friends whilst the young John William was being cared for by his father and a succession of nurse maids. We get some idea of his early life from his father's diaries:

1828.

Oct. 9th. *Jonkey's (sixth) birthday. We had roast beef and plum pudding.*

Oct. 11th. *John had a nasty fall down the opening where the front stairs are to be.*

1829.

Feb. 5th. *The stonemasons returned to their work again having been absent about a fortnight on account of the frost.*

March 2nd. *Commenced preparing the library for wainscoting.*

March 3rd. *Shrove Tuesday. We did not forget to have pancakes.*

Twelve servants were employed in the house to look after the family. John William was followed by four sisters and had to wait until he was eight for his first brother, Ralph Debank, to be born. Ralph was followed by Susanna who was later, after a tragically short marriage, to become housekeeper and life-long companion to John William when his wife died shortly after the birth of his only child Ralph De Tunstall.

Though bitter family feuds and other tragedies were to mar his later years, his childhood and early adult life were comfortable and fulfilling, and, as far as can be seen, happy. His large family of brothers and sisters and the extended family of aunts, uncles and cousins, provided a warm and supportive environment. Servants cared for his every need. His father had carriages with the Sneyd coat of arms emblazoned on them; John William had his own pony and later a horse. There were endless social calls, balls, assemblies, archery parties and shooting on the moors. From an early age he accompanied his father on farm and local business trips, and, like the rest of the family, went to church with him on Sundays.

On the unexpected death of his older brother William on his wedding day, in 1825, the Rev John became heir to the Ashcombe Park estate, and as his eldest son, John William too could now look forward one day to this inheritance. His father further groomed him for his position and, unlike some of his younger brothers, he was not sent away to school but further instructed by his father in estate and judicial matters and sent to board at a local dame school in Leek run by a Mrs Turner. The Rev John records John William's first dinner engagement - at the tender age of seven.

1829

April 3rd *Penelope, John and I dined with Mrs Fowler and attended the playhouse.*

He started school in July of the same year and after he had been there for six days the Rev John noted in his diary, perhaps with some relief:

July 29th *I called on Mrs Turner and saw Jonkey. He appeared very happy.*

John William appears not to have been a natural scholar. His diary shows a casual use of spelling and an almost non-existent use of punctuation. He was essentially a young man of action. He enjoyed the country pursuits of hunting, fishing and riding, and trained with the local volunteer militia with evident enthusiasm and success. He enjoyed making things, and in this respect was like his father and grandfather. Above all, like many of the Sneyd men-folk, he enjoyed shooting; it was in fact a lifelong passion. In 1818, his uncle Ralph had recorded in his diary a list of things shot during six weeks in the autumn of that year:

Partridges, 76; Hares, 21; Rabbits, 19; Pheasants, 3;

Woodcock, 1; Cats, 3; Owl, 1; Pigeon, 1

Some 50 years later his sister Susanna was to record that her brother John William had been shooting with a neighbouring land owner, Sir John Crewe, and in two bloody days they had bagged 400 head of game on the first day and 300 on the next.

John William led a privileged life in his father's house. Like many Church of England ministers at that time, the Rev John did not view his role as evangelical. Though there can be no doubt of his deep belief and commitment to his faith, he saw his duties as being in church on a Sunday and of administering the sacraments of marriage, baptism and internment as required. The rest of his week was taken up with running his extensive farming interests, performing local duties as a JP and magistrate, sitting on road and police committees, leading an active social life, and engaging in business ventures in mining, roads and buying shares in the newly emerging railways with his father and other relatives. His attitude towards the poor in his parish was paternalistic, helping in times of need, supporting local education and inoculations, though much of the day to day work was relegated to his wife and daughters and his curate John Holley, his wife's half brother. Although not in the top echelon of society, and definitely inferior to their relatives at Keele Hall whom they held in some awe, the Sneyd family were people of local importance and influence. The Rev John wrote in 1838:

Aug. 20th.   *Between 20 and 30 gentlemen waited upon me and presented me with a candelabrum and soup tureen and four corner dishes as a reward for my services as a magistrate.*

Magistrates received no fee and the gentlemen who presented this gift must have been satisfied indeed; the amount that they subscribed, and the value of the gift, was recorded by the Rev John in his diary of that year. The gift of silver-ware cost over £350 (£17,500).
Other good things also came his way:

Sept. 6th.   *Mr and Mrs and Miss Kate Cruso, Mr and Mrs Challinor and Mr Ward dined with us. We had a haunch of venison which Mr Watts Russell had been so kind as to give me.*

Whilst landowners like the Sneyds lived very well on their own produce - sheep, cattle, fruit and vegetables, (often from heated greenhouses) - and kept large houses with servants to care for them, their farmworkers and labourers did not. Wages were at near starvation level. With the enclosure acts of the late eighteenth and early nineteenth centuries having robbed them of ancient common grazing rights which enabled them to keep a pig, a few hens or a goose, and with their small allotments on which they grew simple vegetables swallowed up into enclosed estates, and the woodlands from which they had gathered fuel now denied them as were the gleanings from the edges of the fields after harvest, the labourer and his family were in a pitiful state. He had to take whatever work was offered, whatever the rate of pay, and was totally dependent for his miserable existence on the local gentry and farm owners.

The contrast in life styles could hardly have been greater. In his farm accounts for 1829 the Rev John recorded:

Two men at day wages, 12 days together   £1 4s 8d

(about £5 per day each 1995)

A woman for squitching (pulling up couch grass) *for a day*   5d

(about £2.50p per day 1995)

Wages of £5 per hour for a man are barely deemed enough today, let alone £5 for a whole day's work, yet that is what they were paid. The Rev John seemed happy enough to go along with the accepted rate of pay. The Church of England as a whole saw no need to intervene, being part of the landowning class, and it was left to the rising tide of non-conformist churches and the emerging trade union movements to champion the cause of the common man. The mass exodus from villages to rapidly expanding towns was all but unstoppable.

During his lifetime, John William was to see England change irrevocably, and one suspects, from his point of view, for the worse. The industrial revolution and the drift to the towns cut at the very roots of the old assumptions of landed power and prestige. Into the bargain, the affluent life style which he had every hope of enjoying as a young man was to be denied him. The Sneyd family fortunes were already in a perilous state when he was born, but reckless speculation in mining (the ruin of so many families in the nineteenth century), compounded by years of extravagant living and endless disastrous litigation and lawyers fees, robbed him of his hopes.

The friction was not confined to suits against strangers. After a terrible row with his father over money and the mortgaging of the family estates, which was never healed, John William was disinherited. As a result, a bitter feud developed in later years between his brother Dryden Henry, who inherited Ashcombe Park, and him. It ended in acrimonious and futile court cases extending over many years and recrimination and total separation. John William was to repeat the pattern with his only son, allegedly cutting him off when he married unwisely, in John William's eyes. From an affluent and happy childhood, John William was to end his days in bitter isolation and in illness-racked, genteel poverty.

However none of this had happened in 1844, the date of the diary we have before us. He was 22, his fathers right hand man and at peace with his family. In an age before paper qualifications were available on a national level, the proven ability to perform a task was of prime importance. John William was a capable young man who trained as a surveyor and learnt to manage men. He was already in charge of a troop of the local Volunteer Militia and had shown that he could deal effectively with men much older than himself.

The trips that he describes to Wales in this diary are very illuminating. With his father and grandfather, he was a partner in a mine which they had leased on the slopes of Snowdon. It is obvious from his diary that things were not going well. Had he but known it, this speculation was to be the downfall of the family; the venture eventually cost them in excess of £2 million pounds in modern money. They had embarked on it, it would seem, with little advice and by the time they consulted a mining expert, it was too late. Running the business from a distance and without a knowledge of the Welsh language, they were experiencing endless difficulties and as usual with the Sneyd family, they turned to litigation to sort it out. One suspects that the local miners did not take kindly to absentee mine-owners who tried to drive too hard a bargain. The first encounter they had was with the Rev John on his first visit; he introduced himself to them by preaching at them in their cottages half way up Snowdon in a language they did not use - it did not endear him to them!

John William's description of the summer of 1844 is colourful. The whole family set off, on horseback and in carriages, to be in Wales for this great adventure, including the youngest member Gustavus Alfred who was only two months old when his mother braved the arduous journey with him. They went with servants and cart loads of goods, renting a house in the spectacular and beautiful Snowdon foothills from the Rev Vaudrey for £65 a year (£3,500). Relatives descended upon them, and the almost unquenchable energy of the family is recorded in their walks, including ones to the summit of Snowdon, their boat trips, sightseeing, fishing and other forays into the local community, including visits to church every week, taking tea and going to the fair at the nearest village of Beddgelert. How tragic then that within six years all this was to be gone. John William would be totally estranged from his father, the family fortunes would be in tatters and Penelope, his mother, dead.

Sunday 21st January
Read the morning and evening prayers
and two sermons to the Colony

Page from the Diary of the Rev John Sneyd for 1844

Editors' notes

The spelling in the diary which follows has been left as John William wrote it except for place names which have been changed to the accepted spelling for the sake of clarity. Similarly, the puncuation is John William's unless the meaning is unclear in which case punctuation is added thus [,]. Since he was using a small (10cm x 16cm) printed diary with only seven narrow lines to each day, he often used initials instead of full names. The following list identifies people mentioned by initials.

Uncle J	Uncle John Holley, his mother's half brother, who was his father's curate at Ipstones.
Uncle H	Uncle Henry his father's brother, who was perpetual curate of Wetley Rocks.
H	Sister Harriet, born in 1824.
EJ	Sister Emily Jane, born in 1825.
PM	Sister Penelope Marianne, born in 1826.
RD	Brother Ralph Debank, born in 1830.
S	Sister Susanna, born in 1831.
DH	Brother Dryden Henry, born in 1833.
M	Sister Mary Elizabeth, born in 1835.
EL or L	Brother Edmund Lionel, born 1837. Always called Lionel in the family.
FC	Brother Frederick Clement, born 1839.
GA	Brother Gustavus Alfred, born June 1844.

John William's sister Helen, born in 1828, died in february 1844, and he had another brother, Richard Wettenhall, born 1841, who was an invalid and does not feature in the diary.

Captain P	Captain Powys, a locally important land-owner with whom the Rev John had frequent and violent disagreements.
WB	William Blunt, see below.

Other people mentioned in the diaries are:

Mr Ackers	Captain Ackers of the Staffordshire Yeomanry, who served with John William.
Mary Adderley	Daughter of Ralph Adderley of Barlaston Hall.
Mrs Blore	A servant.
William Blunt	The Sneyd's coachman.
Mr Challinor	Solicitor and family friends. The firm was to represent the family for many years and their plate can still be seen in Derby Street, Leek.
Mr Cruso	A local Solicitor and personal friend. He had a fine house in the Market Place in Leek.
Fanny	Fanny Clowes, under-nursemaid to the Sneyds.
Messrs. Sutton, Flint & Heaton	Local 'surgeons' who acted as both doctor and dentist.
Mr Foudrinier	Owner of the local paper mill in Cheddleton.
Richard Gaunt	
Mr & Mrs Nixon	Undertakers and family friends who lived in Leek
Sir Thomas & Lady Shepherd	Close friends of John William's grandfather. They lived at Crakemarsh Hall, near Uttoxeter.
The Tattons	Tenant farmers on the estate.
Mr Trubshaw	James Trubshaw Junior, a local Surveyor, architect and designer. He built Ashcombe, oversaw the rebuilding of Basford Hall, built the engine house for the mine in Wales and did a lot of other work for the Sneyds. Five generations of Trubshaws were architects in Staffordshire, James Junior being the most famous, having worked on Buckingham Palace.
Whiston	A tenant farmer on the estate.

Many other friends, relatives, neighbours and business colleagues are mentioned in the diary, but it would be tedious to list them all. *(Sic)* in brackets following a word in the diary indicates that this was the actual, if clearly incorrect spelling used by John William.

1844
A year in the life of

JOHN WILLIAM SNEYD
of
BASFORD HALL

John William Sneyd in his Yeomanry uniform, in the yard at Basford c1844.
Artist unknown

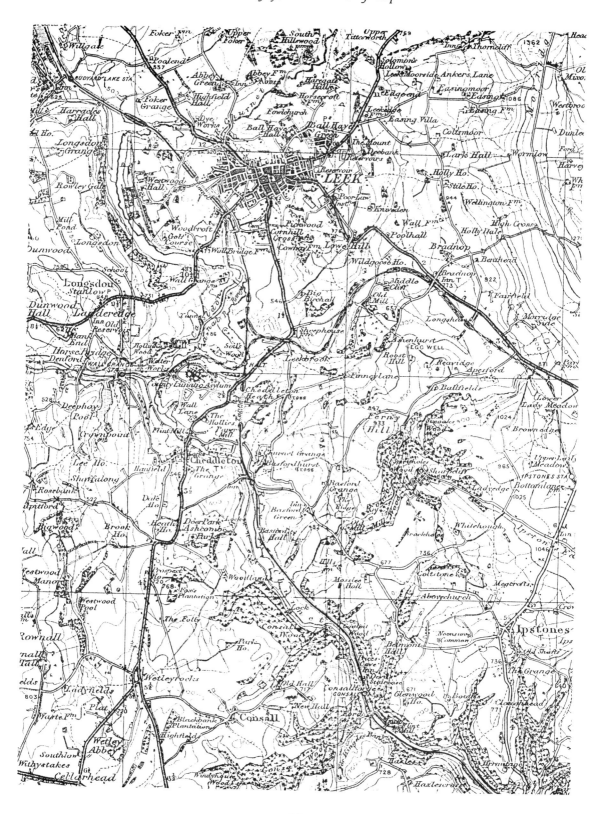

January

1st January

I went collecting on my mare to Old Basford and looked at some of the Roads in the morning and stayed at home in the afternoon It snowed

2nd January

My Father Mother Harriet and I dined at Ashcombe
Sir Thos and Lady Shepherd and Aunt Mary were there

Basford Hall is just outside Cheddleton. It was completely rebuilt by Rev John Sneyd in the 1820s to plans made by the architect James Trubshaw Junior. This painting dates from c1830, and the figures in the foreground are probably Penelope Sneyd, Rev John's wife, and John William, aged about eight. The house still stands and is largely unaltered.
Artist unknown

Ashcombe Park, near Cheddleton. This house was built by William Sneyd, John William's grandfather, on the site of an earlier house called Bottom Hall. The architect was James Trubshaw Junior and building commenced in 1807. Some of the timber came from the estate. In April 1807, William recorded in his diary that he had marked 36 oaks for use in the building of Ashcombe. Unfortunately, his diaries are missing for the period 1808 to 1820, so we do not have any further information about the progress of the building. The house still stands and is largely unaltered.

3rd January

My Father went to Leek My Mother Harriet EJ and I went to Ashbowen on our way to the Derby Ball as we thought but it was put off on account of Sir G Crews death We all stayed at Mrs Hare['s]

4th January

Breakfasted at Mr Geffs We all came home again

Portrait of Rev John Sneyd, (1798-1873), John William's father. John Sneyd was educated at Brasenose College, Oxford, and took Holy Orders. In 1822 he married his cousin, Penelope Holley, and later that year moved to Odstone in Leicestershire as curate. John William was born that October. Two years later Rev John returned to Staffordshire. He rebuilt Basford Hall as his family home. He became heir to the Ashcombe estate the following year, on the death of his brother William. In 1833 he became 'perpetual curate' of Ipstones, and remained incumbent there until 1861, when he resigned. According to local legend, the Bishop requested his resignation because of his high-handed treatment of a drunken parishioner who was "impertinent" to him. He was an energetic and ambitious man, active as a magistrate and on local committees. He established a school at Ipstones in 1834 and built a church at Foxt.

Left: John William's sister Emily Jane (1825-1901), probably painted in the 1840s. Emily Jane remained a spinster and spent most of her life in the Cheddleton area. Latterly she lived at Rose Cottage, Bradnop.

Right: John William's sister Harriet (1824-57), painted c1838 when she would have been 14 years old. She married Rev Robert Bamford, Vicar of Mickleton in Gloucestershire in 1850, and had four children, Penelope Dorothea "Dora", born 1851, Harriet, born 1853, Robert, born 1854 and William Henry, born 1856.

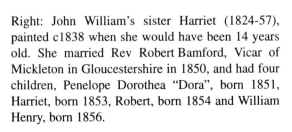

5th January

It was very wet all day.

6th January

My Father Harriet & Ralph rode to Cheadle my Father on my mare Harriet on Cathlene Ralph on David I stayed about home   (Cathlene and David were horses.)

7th January

My Father went to Foxt in the morning & Ipstones in the afternoon I stayed at home in the house

SALE AT IPSTONES,
INSTEAD OF THE
ASSEMBLY ROOM, SWAN INN, LEEK.

MR HILLIARD

BEGS to inform the Gentry and Public of Leek and neighbourhood, that the Sale of very valuable HOUSEHOLD FURNITURE, excellent Library of BOOKS, GLASS, CHINA, EARTHENWARE, KITCHEN REQUISITES, BREWING UTENSILS, and other Effects, advertised to be Sold by Auction, in the Swan Inn Assembly Room, Leek, on Thursday and Friday, the 28th and 29th days of December, 1843, *will take place on the Premises of the owner, P. Langley, Esq. Surgeon, Ipstones, on Monday and Tuesday, the 8th and 9th days of January*, 1844.

N.B.—Printed Particulars are now ready, and may be had by applying to Mr HILLIARD, Market Place, Leek.

HANDSOME, GENTEEL, AND VALUABLE

HOUSEHOLD FURNITURE, &c.

TO BE SOLD BY AUCTION,

By Mr Hilliard,

(Without reserve) in the *Queen's Head Inn Yard, Custard Street, Leek,* in the county of Stafford, on *Monday* and *Tuesday,* the 15th and 16th days of *January,* 1844;

THE truly excellent, modern, valuable and useful Household Furniture, Books, Linen, Glass, China, Earthenware, Brewing Utensils, Kitchen Requisites, and other Effects, on the Premises of Mr CHARLES SMITH, Draper.

N.B.—Catalogues will be distributed in due time, and may be had on application to Mr Hilliard, Market-place, Leek.

8th January

My Father and Ralph walked to Ipstones to Mr Langleys sale I stayed at home

Advertisement for auction sales to be held at Ipstones and Leek.
North Staffordshire Mercury Saturday January 8th 1844.

9th January
*My Father & Ralph went in the gig
to Mixon Hay in the morning My
Father Mother & EJ dined at
Foxearth I s[t]ayed in the house
with a bad cough almost all day*

A gig such as John William drove

Mixon Hay was one of the Rev John's estates up on the moors. In May of 1844 he paid a bill of £84 7s 2d - approximately £4,224 in today's money - to a firm of solicitors called Worthington and Hamilton for work they had done on arranging a mortgage on the estate. Possibly this represented a percentage of the money he had raised, which was probably needed to finance the mining work in Wales.

10th January
*I stayed in the house all day with a bad
cough My Father stayed about home*

11th January
*I stayed in the house making maps all
day*

12th January
*My Father went to Cheadle about the
map of consal parish I coppied (sic) some
maps.*

13th January
*I stayed in the house coppiing (sic) maps Mr
Sutton came to see Helen and I*

Portrait of William Sneyd (1767-1850), John William's grandfather, who at this time owned the estate which John William and his father were so carefully mapping

14th January
It was morning [service] at Ipstones

15th January
I stayed in the house all day

16th January
My Father Mother and most of [my] sisters went to Cheadle to see cousin Caroline married We were to have gone to dance at Dilhorn but we did not go because Helen was poorly I stayed in the house all day

17th January
My Father went to the justice meeting [,] called to ask after Mr Cruso Mr Leigh and to se[e] Mr Heaton

Trentham 1844

18th January
My Father and Ralph went to an agricultural meeting at Trentham in the gig and from thence to se[e] the Bishop and then onto Mathas on their way into Wales

19th January
I stayed about home all day tis very wet windy and cold

20th January
I stayed in the house all day it was very fine and mild

21st January
I stayed in the house all day

22nd January
I stayed in the house all day

23rd January
I rode to Leek to ask the Sergeant Major to come to kill some rabbits

24th January
I went out shooting with Sergeant Major Dean and Whiston and killed 1 Woodcock 3 Pheasants and 5 Rabbits.

Late 19th century steel engraving of a sportsman, contained in a scrap book which John William's son Ralph De Tunstall Sneyd kept as a child. *Reproduced by courtesy of Keele University Library*

25th January
I went rabbiting with S M Dean and Whiston and killed 10 Mr Sutton and Mr Flint came to see Helen I shot at a mark with a carbine.

26th January
I rode to Bagnal to try to induce some young men to join the Yeomanry Mr Cape came to put a pully (sic) to tighten one of the straps on the building and to put the straw cutter in order

27th January
Mr Sutton came to se[e] Helen I rode to Leek to enquire how Mr Cruso was and called at Ashcombe on my way home

A straw cutter

28th January
I stayed in the house all day

29th January
My Father & Ralph came home from out of Wales I stayed in the house almost all day

30th January
My Father & Ralph walked to Ashcomb Uncle Henry called to se[e]Helen Mr Flint called to se[e] her

31st January
Helen was a great deal worse Mr Sutton came

A country lane

February

The death of his sixteen year old sister from comsumption was a trauma for the whole family. Helen was the first of the children to die. Unhappily a further five were to die as young adults, three of them from consumption. Rev John Sneyd was in Wales when Helen became worse. John William sent a message to his father, which somehow reached him halfway up Snowdon. The Rev John set out at once the next morning in a carriage with Ralph Debank, aged 14, who was with him. In the depth of winter and on unmetalled roads they travelled hard and covered the usual three day journey in two days. When he got home the Rev John spent day and night by his daughter's bedside. but she died just five days later. On her death bed Helen had given everyone a memento to remember her by. As a young girl with no income, all she had to give were things she had made or been given. To her
mother she gave her prayer book.

1st February
My Dear sister gave my Father a companion to the altar She gave each of us something She gave me a little box in the shape of a shoe and a pincusheon [made] with her own hands

Her father, Rev John Sneyd, recorded in his diary;
"my dear Angelic child Helen died at about 6 o'clock this evening. She made me a present of the Bible given to her by Mrs Moreton."

2nd February
My Dear Sister Helen died at about $1/4$ past 6 in the evening Mr Sutton came in the morning Ralph has a pain in his chest and has been bled with leeches.

3rd February
Ralph had a blister on his chest and stayed in bed all day

4th February
We all stayed in the house all day

5th & 6th February
My Father and I walked to Ashcombe

7th February
We all stayed in the house

8th February
My Dear Sister Helen was buried in the vault at Ipstones My Father Uncle[s] T & H and I went in the morning coach 7 of the women servants and Mrs Nixon were berers (sic) There were fore (sic) horses to the close cariage My Mare ....

This illustration comes form a popular mid-nineteenth century book "Orange Blossoms" by T S Arthur, which gave advice to young women on how to be perfect wives and mothers. Death was an important part of every family's experience, and they needed to know how to deal with it.

Her father descibed the funeral;
"*The earthly remains of my Darling Helen were removed to the Family vault at lpstones. My brothers Tom and Henry, John William and I were the Mourners. 7 of my female servants and Mrs Nixon dressed in white were the bearers .....*"

It is interesting that none of her sisters, her aunts or her Mother attended the funeral and that the female servants who attended her were dressed in white. The Landon Band played and the funeral coaches were draped in black. Her coffin alone cost £11, the equivalent of over £1000 today, and altogether, as the accounts at the back of the Rev John's diary show, the funeral cost well over the equivalent of £4,000.

Mrs Nixon for post boys and drivers, etc. for poor Helen's funeral	£ 1-1s-0d
The Landon Band	£ 5-0s-0d
Envelopes and stamps	3s-0d
William and Jasper Nixon, joiners for poor Helen's funeral	£11-0s-0d
For dear Helen's funeral	£17-0s-0d
Mr Adderley -do-	£ 1-1s-6d
Ralph Critchlow for opening the vault	5s-0d

Helen's funeral was also to be the occasion of the healing of a family feud which had arisen over Rev John's mother's will.
Feb 5th
Wrote to my brother Tom a letter of reconciliation & invited him to the Funeral of my dear Helen.

Poor Helen had received the best medical attention that money could buy, but there were no antibiotics, and consumption was the scourge of rich and poor alike. Calomel, which had been prescribed for her and which was a very widely taken medicine, was in itself dangerous, being a compound of mercuric oxide. It was later discovered to cause fever, rashes, and enlargement of the spleen and lymph nodes, and by the end of the century had been phased out. But in 1844 the remedies available to any doctor were few indeed.

Helen's memorial can be seen in Ipstones church.

Late 19th century funeral card

9th February

We all stayed in the house all day except my Father and I walked to Mr Nixons

a large party of fashionables enjoyed
the sport of shooting by hundreds all manner of pheasants and partriges

Shooting was to become a life long passion with John William. This becomes increasingly apparent as the diary unfolds throughout the seasons. This illustration is taken from *Richard Doyle's Diary*, September 2nd 1840. Doyle later worked for Punch magazine.

10th February

Whiston and I went out rabbiting and killed a great many snipe

11th February

We almost all of us went to Ipstones in the morning

12th February

My Father and I walked to Leek and called to se (sic) Mr Cruso Uncle and Aunt Tom called

13th February

I stayed about home all day

from Miller's Olde Leeke

14th February
My Father and I walked to Leek and came back by Ashcombe

St Leonard's Church, Ipstones.

The church was built betwen 1787 and 1792 by John Sneyd of Belmont Hall, John William's great grandfather. Rev John Sneyd, John William's father, was "perpetual curate" of Ipstones from 1833-1861. The family regularly travelled the four uphill miles from Basford Hall to Ipstones to attend the church. The church was renovated and enlarged in 1877, and again in 1902-3, when the porch was added

Photograph W Nithsdale

15th February

I stayed about home all day

16th February

My Father and I stayed about home all day

Gig

17th February

I went to the paddock shooting with Whiston

Although he did drive, unless they were going a considerable distance walking was the way most favoured by the Rev John of getting from one place to another. John William preferred riding or driving and often drove his mother, sisters and brothers. He seems to have been a keen and competent horseman.

18th February

My Father went in the gig to Ipstones in the morning on his way to Foxt

20th February

I went to see the men getting gravel out of the Combs Brook for the use of the roads

21st February

My Father Miss Bereham and 4 sisters walked to Leek I rode and walked with my Father to see Mr Davenport Snr at Westwood Harriet was taken ill

The Lithograph

Foxt Church, built in 1839 by Rev John Sneyd at his own expense, to serve this outlying part of his parish. He recorded the making of this illustration:

	£	s.	d.
"Gave Mr MacDougal for drawing Foxt Church	3	12	6
and his expenses in ordering the lithograph."	5	0	6
	8	13	0

28

Westwood Hall, c1835, belonged to John Davenport (1765-1848). From humble beginnings he had risen to become owner of his own pottery and glass works at Longton. He acquired Westwood in 1813 and set about repairing the house and improving and extending the estate. His son, also John Davenport, built a new house on the site after 1851.

Lithograph by W L Walton from Staffordshire Views, courtesy of the William Salt Library.

22nd February
I stayed at home almost all day

23rd February
My Father was at Heaton all day on the Bulls business I walked to Belmont

We do not know what the "Bull's business" was, but a Joseph Ball had lent William Sneyd £500 in 1842. John William's spelling is chaotic and another entry on April 6th refers to the Ball's affairs. It is probable that they were one and the same, and that the business was connected with the loan.

24th February
We had foot drill at Tattons There were ten men at the drill

25th February
We all stayed at home all day

26th February
My Father walked to Ashcombe Ralph rode to to Cheadle and I went to se [e] the roads

27th February
I drove Penelope as far as Highfields in the gig and I went on to Loxley where I met cousins Miss and Rosa Cave & Mary Adderley We danced in the evening & cousins played and sang

Penelope Marianne Sneyd (1826-77) was John William's third sister. In 1848 she married John Clerk Brodie of Idvies, Angus, who was Crown Agent for Scotland, and they had a large family. Here she is pictured standing on the Bath House terrace at Basford Hall, and is carrying an archery bow.

Songs were often published in papers and magazines. Young women made their own copies, for they were expected to be able to entertain. This seems to have been a happy five days after the sadness earlier in the month.

28th February

I walked with Miss Cave to Uttoxeter & called at Highfields We danced in the evening and cousins played and sang

29th February

We all dined at Highfields Mary Adderley played and sang It was Mary Adderleys birthday

Highfields Hall was near Uttoxeter. It was the home of the Rev John's sister, Mary Sneyd Kynnersley, John William's Aunt Mary, and her children. Today there is a residential home for the elderly on the site of the Hall.
Reproduced by courtesy of Staffordshire Museum Service.

High Street, Uttoxeter.

The family visited Uttoxeter regularly. They had relatives at both Loxley Park and Highfields with whom they often stayed. These postcards show Uttoxeter as it was at the turn of the century. It had changed little since John William's day.

Market Place, Market Day, Uttoxeter

March

1st March
*I was in the shop all day We danced in the evening and cousins played
and sang*

3rd March
*We went to Uttoxeter church in the morning and went a walk with Uncle
Kynnersley in the afternoon*

Barlaston Hall c1830. It was rebuilt c1756-8, by Thomas Mills, attorney, of Leek, who married an heiress of the Bagnall family. By 1822 it had passed to Rosamund Mills, who lived there with her husband Ralph Adderley and their children, including Mary. In 1849 Francis Wedgwood moved to the Lea estate at Barlaston, and by the second half of the 19th century the Wedgwoods had taken over from the Adderleys as the chief family in Barlaston. The house still stands and now belongs to Wedgwood.

Huntley Hall (above) was the home of John William's grandfather's younger brother, Rear Admiral Clement Sneyd RN (1773-1854). He married Helen Swettenham of Somerford Booths, Cheshire, by whom he had two sons and two daughters, and secondly Elizabeth Cotton of Etwall Hall, Debyshire. In 1861, John William married her kinswoman, Agnes Cotton, also of Etwall Hall

5th March
The Caves and Mary Adderley went to Barlaston I came home and called at Huntley

Etwall Hall in Derbyshire

MYSTERIOUS AFFAIR.

On Wednesday, the 6th instant, an inquest was held by Mr Cattlow, at Calton Moor House, between Leek and Ashbourne, on the body of a female, whose name is unknown, and who died on the 4th instant. She came there on the 17th ult., dressed in male attire, and remained in consequence of indisposition. — She stated her name to be Arthur Fitzherbert, and had letters written to persons bearing that name in Ireland, but no answers have been received. On the 25th ult., it was discovered that she was a female, and she then said that her mother's name was Newton, and that she lived at Macclesfield. She also referred to a lady in Devonshire, who, she said, had befriended her, and to whom a letter has been addressed. The deceased is about five feet high, has dark grey eyes, dark hair rather inclining to auburn, teeth very white and regular, a fair complexion, and a slight scar near the left eye and under the eye-brow. While she remained disguised, she stated that she was seventeen years of age, but after the discovery, said she was twenty-two, and she appears to be somewhat older.

She gave to the daughter of the landlord, a new octavo prayer book, handsomely bound, printed at Oxford, in 1839, and bearing the following inscription, apparently in a female hand, on one of the blank pages :—

" To a friend, from one who wishes them the spiritual " blessings.—Jan. 29th, 1844."

The deceased had previously been in the same disguise for several days, at the Green Man, at Ashbourne, and at the Isaac Walton, at Dovedale ; at both of which places she paid for what she had, but when she came to Colton Moor House, she had only two shillings.

The jury found that the deceased died of Bronchitis, and the body will be interred to day or on Sunday. In the mean time it will remain at Calton Moor House, to afford an opportunity for any friends to identify it.

THE INQUEST. - *"The body having been viewed, and all the prelimineries gone through, the examination of the witnesses commenced."*   *from "Mind Whom You Marry" Rev C G Rowe,*

The *North Staffordshire Mercury,* Saturday 9th March 1844, reported the inquest of a young woman who had been travelling dressed as a young man. John William's father had attended this inquest, but though John William referred to it, he made no mention of the peculiarity of the case. Such omissions are common in all the Sneyd diaries, making us wonder what other information may be lacking.

6th March
My Father and I walked to the Paddock in the morning My Father went to an inquest at Carlton moor House in the afternoon

7th March
My Father and I walked to the Padewick farm

8th March
My Father and Mr Tatton walked to Garston to see some draining the former went up to Mixon Hay and Mr Bakers My Father gave R Baker leave to shoot over the common at Onecote & Bradnop and all his farms there

9th March
My Father and I looked over the books in the library

10th March
My Father and I went to Ipstones in the morning

11th March
My Father and I went in the gig to Cheadle there was some business to be done concerning the Superintendant of Pollice (sic) and a constable

13th March
My Father and I went Leek in the gig

14th March
I rode to se(sic) some men repairing the roads and to pay for stone of different people

15th March
I went out rabbiting with Whiston and killed 4

16th March
My Father stayed at home EJ and I walked to Ashcombe

17th March
My Father went to Foxt in the morning EJ and I went to Ipstones in the afternoon

18th March
Mrs Brindley and Miss Ibthanson spent the day here Mrs Child called My Father Uncle John Lionel JC & I called at Ashcombe

19th March
Mr F Cruso called I went to Rownal to collect Shaws rate

20th March
My Father and I went to Leek and called at Ashcombe

Advertisements for dentistry from *North Staffordshire Mercury*, 1844. All the Sneyds seem to have suffered with poor teeth. Mr Sutton was the local surgeon. At this time there was no national Examination or recognised qualification. He would probably have gained his knowledge by working as an apprentice to a qualified doctor for several years. He was used by the Sneyd family for a very long time, so he must have given satisfaction.

21st March
Aunt Mary came to spend the day

22nd March
My Father and I went to the Borde (sic) and called and dined at Rownal Mr Sutton came and pulled out 2 of FC teeth and 1 of EJ

"Borde" probably means the Board of Guardians, the body which was concerned with poor relief.

Aunt Mary

Aunt Mary was John William's father's younger sister. She married Clement John Sneyd-Kynnersley in 1830, and lived at Highfields, near Uttoxeter. She had two sons and a daughter, but was widowed in 1840. She remained very close to her brother, and to her nephews and nieces. Letters show her to have been kind and gentle and the family peacemaker.

23rd March
My Father and I stayed about home

24th March
My Father and I went to Ipstones in the morning

25th March
Uncle and Aunt Tom called My Father EJ Uncle Tom & I dined at Ashcombe

26th March
Mr Sutton came to se (sic) Mama
John William's mother was pregnant with her thirteenth and last child.

St Edward Street, Leek.
From an etching by Mackarness, c1890

27th March
I went to Leek with my Father

28th March
I made up my road accounts and attended a meeting to have them examined

29th March
I stayed about home all day My Father went to Ashcombe

As the volume of traffic on the country's roads had increased, turnpike trusts had been set up to levy tolls on passing vehicles. These tolls were used to repair and improve the roads, but individual trustees also profited from them. Both John William's father and grandfather were also turnpike trustees.

30th March

I was down at the building turning a trencher which I gave to Aunt Mary I took a ride in the afternoon

The 'building' was a workshop. John William, like his father, loved to make things. He was a practical man, not a scholar. The illustration shows the process he used with a foot lathe.

Illustrations of lathe and trencher are taken from *Little Ladder of Learning,* Anon, undated.

31st

My Father and I went to Foxt in the morning & Ipstones in the afternoon

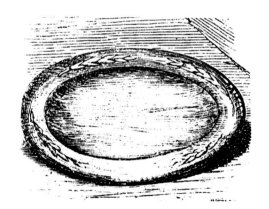

A wooden trencher

April

1st April
Edmond Lionels birthday

2nd April
Harriet went to Woodlands to stay a few days. Mr Sutton came.

Members of the newly established, uniformed London police force, from a cartoon by Leech
Punch, 1851

3rd April
My Father and I went to the Justice meeting at Leek. Captain P Mr Meigh Mr H met him there they did not agre (sic) about Mills being a constable CP challenged my Father.

The Rev John's account of this meeting is even more direct; *'had a row with Captain Powys about the appointment of constables.'* The row was to rumble on for several months with both men drumming up support for their case. Unrest was rife in the Country and had been for seveal years, due to the very low wages and the high cost of basic food. Riots had taken place in Stoke on Trent two years earlier and the volunteer militia had been brought in to quell them. Arson was widespread and the feeling was that far greater numbers of police were needed. In London a uniformed force was being established. But greater power in police hands meant less power in the hands of the Magistrates who, for generations, had been the most powerful men in their area and represented the landed classes and the 'old order'. The Rev John and Captain Powys seem to typify the acrimonious division over the direction that the appointment of officers of law and order should take, which was countrywide at this time.

BURNING OF ALBION HOUSE, SHELTON—THE RESIDENCE OF WILLIAM PARKER, ESQ.

Riots in Stoke-on-Trent, 1842

4th April
RD DH & Wintle a friend of Ralphs came home for the Easter Holiday

5th April
My Father went to Foxt in the morning I drove H. Wintle in the Gig in the afternoon to Ipstones

6th April
My Father went to Ipstones on the Balls business. Uncle John JH EJ DH dine[d] and spent the day at Belmont.

Belmont Hall was built by John William's great grandfather, John Sneyd. He was a keen horticulturalist, and his planting of the gardens at Belmont was much praised. Loudon described it as '*a place combining the justest taste, great knowledge of culture, agricultural as well as horticultural, and a strict regard in all things to economy in the first expence (sic) and future management"*

(Illustrations of Landscape Gardens and Garden Architecture by J.C.Loudon, 1830)

Belmont was the home of the Rev John's brother Thomas and his wife, Emma, John William's "Uncle and Aunt Tom". The Rev John had lived at Belmont himself as a young man, when he was the pupil of the Rev Carlisle who then rented the Hall from the Sneyds.

Much of the planting remains and the house still stands, but is much altered.

7th April

I rode to Church in the morning on my mare and attended the sacrament My Father went to Foxt in the afternoon.

Shire Hall and Market Place, Stafford, in the mid 19th century. Built by John Harvey, 1759, the Hall contains the now disused court room where John William attended with his father. The courts were extended in the 1850's and survive in that form, though they are no longer used. Shire Hall connected with the Judge's House, built c1800, where John William and his father sometimes dined.

8th April

I went with my Father to Leek where he swore in some constables RD & Mr Wintle went with us all on horse back.

9th April

My Father and I went to Stone in the Gig where we attended an agricultural meeting & preseded (sic) from there on to Stafford and dined at JS. [The Judge's House]

10th April

I was in court all day & Heard my Father try some prisoners & dined & had tea at the Judges Lodgings

11th April

I was in court till ½ past 4 when I left my Father on his way into Wales I drove Mr Harland in the Gig to Sandon & stayed the night there. Ralph and Dryden went back to school.

Old Houses, Greengate Street, Stafford c1859

12th April
I came home from Sandon in the Gig by myself.

13th April
I attended a Horse drill at Ipstones there were 20 preasent (sic) from there on to Stafford and dined at JS

14th April
I rode my mare to Ipstones in the afternoon

15th April
Harriet EJ & I went in the Faitent [phaeton] to Loxley We called at Huntley.

16th April
I turned some blood sticks and a Box & Walked to Highfields with Aunt Mary & Susan and returned in the Highfields Pony Cariage (sic)

Despite extensive enquiries the use of blood sticks remains a mystery.

17th April

Uncle & Aunt Tom called. I went with Uncle Kynersley to the Justice meeting at Utoxeter & called at Heath House for a Neopolitan pig on my way home

18th April

I have been sawing wood almost all day for pales by the Stues (sic) Mr & Miss Flint called

"Stues" were stews or fishponds containing fish for the table.

19th April

Uncle John & I went up to the moors in the Gig snipe shooting

20th April

I rode to Cheddleton on my mare to ask if we could have 2 horse loads of lime to plaster Mrs Blores room My Father left Wales for home

21st April

I went to Ipstones in the morning on my horse My Father stayed at Shrewsbury all day

22nd April

My Father came home from out of Wales having come from Shrewsbury Mr & Mrs Fisher brought him from Handley

Shrewsbury castle c1893, Photograph from *"Beautiful Britain.*

23rd April
I took the two pointers Gell & Snap to their Walks at the Home Farms My Father H. EJ. & I dined at Ashcombe & met Sir Ths and Lady Shepwerd there.

24th April
My Father and I went Leek I had my surveyors accounts looked verified.

25th April
I went in the Gig to Morton Hall to stay two nights

26th April
I took a walk with Mr. Ackers and looked over the house he is building

27th April
I came home from Morton Hall

28th April
I went in the Gig as far as Ipstones with my Father on our way to Foxt in the morning and walked from thence

29th April

I attended a Horse drill at Leek There were about 20 or 30 preasent (sic) I had the command My Father went with me

30th April

We almost all of us spent the day at Belmont

Sneyd
Nec Opprimre Nec Opprimi

Arms of Dryden Sneyd, incorporating the twelve shields of the various branches of the Sneyd family and the Sneyd crest and motto.

from Sleigh's *History of the Ancient Parish of Leek*

May

1st May
We all went to Leek to see Mr.Van Amburg We some of us had tee(sic) at Mrs. Brindleys the others at Mr F Crusos

2nd May
I went to the Turnpike road to see Van Amburg drive 8 horses

Pottery figure of Isaac Van Amburgh, made in Staffordshire c1842/4. Van Amburgh had also visited Newcastle-under-Lyme in December 1842. It is a pity that John William does not tell us more about the act. One of Van Amburgh's performances involved ascending in a flood-lit balloon with his leopard; presumably he did not do this in Leek or one of the Sneyds would surely have recorded it.

Reproduced by kind permission of the Borough Museum, Newcastle-under-Lyme

Advertisement for a performance by Mr Van Amburgh in Liverpool in March 1844. He was a celebrated circus entertainer who performed equestrian feats and tamed wild animals. John William went to see him twice in Leek in May. This was presumably part of the same tour. John William, a keen horseman himself, seems to have been most interested in the equestrian part of the act.

Van Amburgh was an American who had made his name in 1833 in America when he entered a lion's cage. He was to gain notoriety in 1837 when, as part of his act, he put his head in a lion's mouth. Public sensitivity was offended.

In 1838 he came to England and starred with Ducrow in the famous Astley Circus in London. Mr Astley is credited with teaching Van Amburgh his equestrian skills. The young Queen Victoria was so impressed that she paid six visits to see him perform in January and February 1839. Travelling circuses and caged animal shows were extremely popular at this time. The famous showman Wombwell toured the length and breadth of the country, with up to fourteen caravans of animals, some of which were dragged into the towns by elephants.

In 1840 Van Amburgh and Ducrow set up their own travelling show, but Van Amburgh also travelled alone. He was at the height of his fame in 1844, when he visited Leek as part of a national tour. No record of this seems to have survived in the local archives, but fortunately both John William and the Rev John recorded it in their diaries.

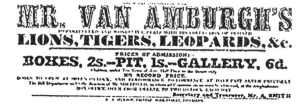

Reproduced by courtesy of the British Library

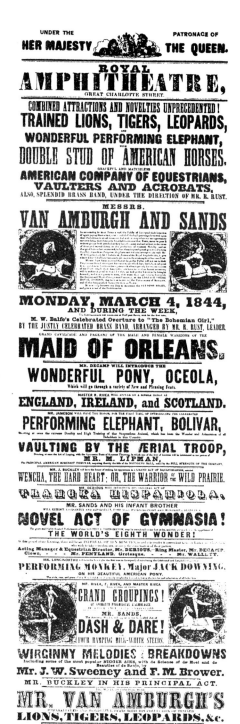

3rd May
Mr Foudrinia & Mr Sutton called

5th May
My Father H EJ S EL & I went to Ipstones Church in the morning My Father went on to Foxt Mr Powys called in the evening.

6th May
I attended a Drill at Leek Captain Ackers attended My Father went with me. I signed the Leek petition against there being any additional Police

Astley's Riding School in 1770.

Astley, with whom Van Amburgh had worked, came originally from Newcastle-under-Lyme. This illustration of his riding school appeared in the *Illustrated London News.*

7th May
Mr Ackers & I attended a Horse drill at Leek . My Father called on Lord Shrewsbury and Mr. Bill.

8th May

I went with my Father to the bord (sic) of Guardians at Leek to get them to sign a petition against having any additional Police

9th May

H & EJ went to Leek in the poney (sic) carriage My Father and I drank tea at Rownall

10th May

My Father and I went to the Bord (sic) of Guardians at Cheadle to get them to sign a petition against addition to the Police Father slept at Rownall

11th May

I rode to Rownall in the morning & went with my Father and Mr Child to Stafford in the Faitent (sic) to oppose an additional Police

There was a paper mill at Cheddleton, owned by a Mr Fourdrinier, who was a friend of the Sneyd family

12th May

My Father went to Foxt in the morning. I went to Ipstones in the afternoon & walked to Ashcombe in the evening & called on Mr. Foudrineau

13th May

Nothing in particular

14th May

Mr. Foudrineau called and also Mr and Mrs Fisher they stayed the afternoon. My Father called at Rownall and Ashcombe

15th May

My Father and I rode to Leek My Father rote (sic) a land letter in the Staffordshire avertiser to Captain Roland Manwaring

16th May

I attended horse drill at Leek. Mr. Ackers was there My Father H. EJ. P.S. EL. JC. went in the Faitent (sic) to Tissington Well dressing They drank tea at Blore

17th May

I attended a horse drill at Leek Mr Ackers was there My Father rode to Cheadle

18th May

I went out Rook Shooting I killed 27 with balls with my little gun My Father stayed at home Mr Basset became the teanant (sic) at the building for £25 a year

19th May

My Father and I went to Ipstons in the morning We lunched with Uncle at Nogin for the first time My Father went on to Foxt.

20th May

I bought a horse of Uncle Tom I gave my mare and £11 for him Uncle and Aunt Tom called I went a ride with them William Blunt took my Grandfathers horse and cart to Wales with them & Fanny and some lugage (sic).

WELL-DRESSING AT TISSINGTON.

Still, Dovedale, yield thy flowers to deck the
    fountains
  Of Tissington upon its holyday;
The customs long preserved among the mountains
    Should not be lightly left to pass away.
They have their moral; and we often may
    Learn from them how our wise forefathers
      wrought,
When they upon the public mind would lay
  Some weighty principle, some maxim brought
Home to their hearts, the healthful product of deep
  thought.'

                        Edwards.

    Such was our feeling when our kind landlady
at Matlock reminded us that on the following
day, being Holy Thursday, or Ascension Day,
there would take place the very ancient and well
kept-up custom of dressing the wells of Tissington
with flowers. She recommended us on no account
to miss the opportunity, 'for the festivity draws
together the rich and poor for many miles round,'
said she; 'and the village looks so pretty you
cannot but admire it.'

The Hall Well, Tissington, as dressed for Ascension Day

An illustration and account published in a contemporary book, *Chambers Book of Days*. In his diary, the Rev John tells who they took tea with, not where. He wrote, *"…….went to Tissington to see the well dressing and we were very kindly received by Sir H and Lady Fitzherbert."*

21st May
I rode my new horse in the eyes and tried him with the sword My Father stayed at home Mr. Sutton came

22nd May
My Father and I rode to Leek we called on Mr Cruso

23rd May
I attended a horse drill at Leek Mr Ackers was there We had a foot drill also I dined with the Crusos with Mr Ackers

24th May
I attended a horse drill at Leek Mr Ackers was there

Officers of the Staffordshire Yeomanry c1860. John William Sneyd is seated in the middle row, second from the left.

Reproduced by courtesy of the Staffordshire Yeomanry collection.

25th May

EJ and I took a ride We went to Ashcombe & round by Leek tolegate

Running at the Heads

26th May

I went to Ipstones Church in the Afternoon Uncle John read prayers and preached my Father being in Wales.

27th May

I let the thre (sic) stues (sic) off & and caught some fish for Uncle John to put in a pit in his ground. I sent him 10.

28th May

EJ & I took a ride To Huntley & came back by Croxlen Abbey & Ipstones

29th May

Uncle John EJ & I rode to Shelton to call on Mr & Mrs Fisher We called at Ashcombe

Running at the Rings

30th May

EJ & I spent the day at Belmont We met Mr & Mrs Coyney Herbert Edward Mrs & 2 Miss Phillips EJ & I rode there on horseback.

Running at the Ball upon the Ground

31st May

I went out rabbit shooting with Dash & killed 4 Mrs Brindley called

John William was an officer with the Staffordshire Yeomanry. A cavalry horse had to undergo various tests to equip it and its rider for battle, as these illustrations demonstrate. The diagrams are taken from *"The Horseman, with sabre exercises for mounted and dismounted services"*, by H R Hershberger, 1844.

Croxden Abbey was a Cistercian abbey, founded in 1176. It is interesting to note that the ruins look much the same today as they did in the 19th century. Then, as now, it was a tourist attraction.

John William's brothers Frederick Clement (1839-64) and Gustavus Alfred (1844-1926), probably photographed about 1860. Frederick Clement, "Feddy", was just five the year John William wrote his diary, and Gustavus, "Tavie" was born that year, in Wales. Frederick died of consumption at the age of twenty five. He was his father's favourite and Rev John was heartbroken at his death. In his diary he gave vent to his deep emotion: "Oct 2nd *My darling son Frederick expired about a quarter before 3 o'clock this morning. O my son Frederick. My son, my son, dearest Fred. Would God that I had died for thee. Oh darling Fred, my son, my son.*" Gustavus became vicar of Chastleton in Oxfordshire. He inherited Basford Hall on John William's death in 1904.

June

1st June

Aunt Tom EJ. Carry & I rode on horseback to Wetton We went by Butterton It was a beautiful ride We stayed tea at Belmont I rode to Ipstones in the morning & lunched with Uncle John

3rd June

Attended a horse Drill at Leek I had the command. EJ & I dined at Mrs Brindleys My Father came home from Wales

4th June

I attended a Horse drill at Leek I had the command My Father rode to Whiston

were ex ercising and fired for the first time this year.

Picture of soldiers drilling, taken from *Richard Doyle's Diary*, 1840.

5th June

My Father Uncle John & I went in the Faitent (sic) to Leek It was the visitation & we attended the justice meeting Mr Trubshaw came home with us from Leek and slept here

Staffordshire Volunteer
CAVALRY.
Religion! Loyalty! and Hi

6th June
Aunt Tom Aunt Mary & Cousin Elisa Kynersley called My Father and Mr Trubshaw went to measure the work at the Paddock stayed about home My Father went to Mixon Hay & Mr Barkers

As a result of the threat of invasion from revolutionary groups in France, volunteer Yeomanry Cavalry divisions were set up throughout the country. John William, like many of the gentry, was an enthusiastic supporter of the Staffordshire group, revelling in the opportunity it gave him to wear a colourful uniform, train with swords and guns, drill foot soldiers and attend social functions.
Reproduced by courtesy of the Staffordshire Yeomanry Collection

7th June
I met Captain Ackers and part of the troop at the top of Basford Lane & went as far as Uttoxeter on our way to Litchfield We joined the Cheadle troop at Uttoxeter My Father went as far as Cheadle

8th June
The Leek & Cheadle Troops marched with a band as far as Hansaham (sic) Bridge where we joined the Uttoxeter troop & we all marched into Litchfield under the command of Captain Ackers I went to the theatre

Lichfield Cathedral

9th June
We all attended the Cathedral in church parade order

10th June
We all went through the field day on Wittington Heath

11th June
We went through the field day as before Captain Ackers & I dined at the Mats &
afterwards went to Mr Chins

12th June

We went through the field day

John William's youngest brother, Gustavus Alfred, was born on June 12th. John William was too busy playing soldiers to record the event. It demonstrates the selective nature of his diary entries.

13th June

We went through the field day and had our arms inspected by Cournel (sic) Steel.

14th June

We were reviewed by Cournel Steel & Capn Ackers went home

15th June

I left Lichfield with the Leek troop at 6 'clock I called at Highfields & Breakfast & had lunch with the troop at Uttoxeter I marched as far as Cheadle with them where I left them to have glass of ale apiece

16th June

I walked with my Father to Ipstones in the morning He went on to Foxt

17th June

My Father & I stayed about Home

18th June

I drove the Gig to Ashbourne to fetch RD & D Henry home for the hollydays (sic) My Father attended Mr Richd Gaunts funeral.

Ralph Debank and Dryden Henry were at school at Ashbourne with the Rev G E Gapp.

19th June

I went with my Father to the Justice meeting at Leek Mr Hatton was there

20th June

We stayed about home

21st June

My Father & I were at Mr. Nixons almost all day My Father committed Bob Bundford for stealing a hat & an other (sic) man for accosting a police man in the execution of his duty My Father & I walked to Ashcombe.

22nd June

I rode with my Father and RD to Stony Slack to look at some papers about the rent of that place it is leased for a thousand years We called at some other houses at Onecote & dined with Mr Bradshaw of Grindon & walked to see the cave near there

23rd June

I rode my horse to Ipstones in the aftrenoon My Father went to Foxt My Father rode Meakin.

25th June

I rode to Whiston & paid some interest for my Grandfather to Mr Scarat and another man My Father and EJ went in the Gig to Stone

William Scarratt had lent £100 to John William's grandfather in 1842. He received interest at the rate of £4 - 10s. per year.

John William was an officer in the Staffordshire Yeomanry as his grandfather, William Sneyd, had been before him. His uniform would have looked like that of the officers in this nearly contemporary picture of The Officers of the Staffordshire Yeomanry Cavalry, c.1853, attributed to H.Marten *Courtesy of the Staffordshire Yeomanry Collection* In 1844, Rev John Sneyd recorded in his accounts:

June	John William for going to Lichfield with the Yeomanry	£10 0 0
July	Thomas Colly for Yeomanry account	£57-0-6
August	John William's Heaton's Cavalry bill	£ 7-8-3¾
December	Subscription to Yeomanry Cavalry dinner	£ 5 0-0

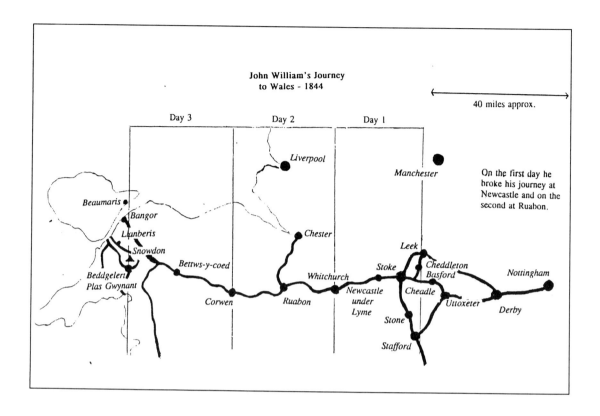

John William's Journey
to Wales - 1844

40 miles approx.

Day 3

Day 2

Day 1

Liverpool

Manchester

On the first day he broke his journey at Newcastle and on the second at Ruabon.

Beaumaris

Bangor

Llanberis

Snowdon

Chester

Leek

Cheddleton

Bettws-y-coed

Stoke

Basford

Nottingham

Beddgelert
Plas Gwynant

Whitchurch

Cheadle

Corwen

Ruabon

Newcastle
under
Lyme

Uttoxeter

Derby

Stone

Stafford

27th June

*I and Sam left Basford at 5 o'clock in the morning
I on my horse & Sam on Meakin for Wales We
baited at W[hitm]oore & Whitchurch &
reached Ruabon My Father RD. DH.EJ.
& William left home by a bote (sic) for
Wales Mr Hips went also*

John William's brother, Dryden Henry
(1833-1913). He inherited Ashcombe Park
on the death of his father in 1873, because
John William had been estranged from his
father since 1852. The brothers were at
loggerheads and spent much time and
money in pointless litigation. This engraving
comes from *"History of the Parish of Leek"*
by John Sleigh, 1883.

28th June
I travailed (sic) from Ruabon baited at Corwen & reached Pentrefoelas I saw a Gentleman named John Car 4 miles this side of Corwen who took a great fancy to my horse

Baited means to rest and feed the horses and themselves. The journey took three days, much of it on toll roads but also on ways that were little more than tracks. With his daughter and two younger boys the Rev John was going by water. In his diary he tells us he went by canal to Runcorn, then by steamer from Runcorn to Liverpool, where he took his children to the Zoological Gardens and to view two American boats before leaving on the packet steamer for Menai Bridge. From there he went by horsedrawn car to Plas Gwynant. His journey, with sightseeing, also took three days.

TOLL-GATE.

Lithograph of Snowdon from Capel Curig. This is a view that John William would have recognised.

29th June
I Travailed from Pentrefoelas baited at Capel Curig & got here My Father RD.DH.EJ. & William came in the night.

30th June
My Father H.PM.S.RD.DH. & I went to church at Beddgelert

July

1st July
My Father & I went to Snodon (sic) in the Poney carriage to se(sic) the mining opperations Mr Bruin drank tea with us

2nd July
My Father & I went to the Snodon mines in the poney carriage William Blunt returned home from Caernarfon with the lugage.

Snowdon and Llanberis Lakes

3rd July

My Father RD & I walked with Mr Williams Gen (sic) over Snodon to view the mines Ordered a level to be commenced at the serface (sic) of the upper lake Took some trout and fishing tackle from a poacher fishing in the middle of the lake

Taken from one of Ralph De Tunstall's scrapbooks
Reproduced by courtesy of Keele University.Library

4th July

My Father RD & I went fishing & only caught one trout Slight rain most of the day

5th July

My Father Mr Trubshaw RD & I went to view the Snowdon mine We went to see the Llanberris Slate Quarries & took tea at the Victoria Inn

6th July

My Father Mr Trubshaw RD & I went to view the Snowdon Mine

7th July

My Father Mr Trubshaw H. PM. RD. S. DH. went to church at Beddgelert

8th July

My Father Mr Trubshaw RD & I went to view the Snodon Mine

9th July
Mr Trubshaw left Mr Bradshaw came

10th July
My Father Mr Bradshaw RD & I went up Snodon We fished part of the day RD caught his first two trout

11th July
My Father & Mr Bradshaw went to call on Mr Ellis & Mr Marsden the clergyman I stayed at home.

12th July
My Grandfather came My Father Mr Bradshaw RD & I went to the mine and we caught 23 fish in the lakes between us.

13th July
My Father RD & I went to Pen-y-Pass It was a very wet day

14th July
My Father & 13 of us went to Beddgelert Church in the afternoon

15th July
My Grand Father My Father RD & I went to the mine at Snodon. My Father Mr Kent & I went to the top it was very clear My Grand Father left here in his carriage for home.

Pass of Llanberis

Disused engine shed at the Snowdon mine. The shed was designed by the Sneyd's architect, James Trubshaw junior, who came down from Staffordshire especially. Six hundred slates were brought from the quarry at Llanberis for the roof. Trubshaw was the architect John Sneyd employed to build Basford Hall. He had also designed Ashcombe Park for William Sneyd, John William's grandfather. Five generations of Trubshaws were architects in Staffordshire. James Junior is the most famous, having worked on Buckingham Palace.   *Photograph Lindsey Porter*

Miner's track across Snowdon, showing 'flat rods' in the distance. These were a method of transmitting power across distances.   *Photograph Lindsey Porter*

17th July
My Father H, PM, went to Bangor in the poney carriage I rode my horse

18th July
My Father & I went to see Mr Williams at Beaumaris to ask him to let us have the lience (sic) of the mine to prove that my Grand Father & I are the partners but he was not at home We went again in the afternoon but he was not come We took tea at Vanol & my Father & I went on to Caernarfon.

Caernarvon Castle

The Rev John Sneyd records in his diary, on the same day, that the case, which was heard in Caernavon, went against them. The lawyer's bill was £112 6s 9d. (about £5,500) and the following month they paid the miners the £286 5s 6½ d (about £14,300) which they said the Sneyds owed to them. We have no record of the number of miners involved but it seems to be huge amount of money given the average wage at that time. Records kept at the Sygon Copper Mine, just outside Beddgelert, at the same period record miners being paid a miserable £2 (£100) a month on average. It could be as high as £8 a month, though this was exceptional, and it could be as low as 10s (£25) a month. The miners at the Sneyd's mine seemed to be getting every penny they could from the inexperienced outsiders, aided, one cannot help thinking, by partisan lawyers who do not seem to have been over-helpful to the Sneyds. Their claim that they had been hired on 'day wage' was probably untrue as miners were almost never hired on these terms as it was a sure recipe for very little work to be done. They were usually paid 'by bargain' which meant that a spokesman for the miners agreed with the owners for a set amount of rock to be mined for a given wage by a set time. On the other side it has to be acknowledged that many of the Sneyd menfolk were arrogant and very litigious. Court cases of every conceivable kind litter their family history. It was only the start of the Sneyds' trouble. They were already in debt to other local tradesmen and law suits followed them well into the next year. In order to get the mine, William Sneyd (John William's grandfather) had paid out £700 (about £35,000) for a part share in it. He had then set up the Snowdon Mining Company with the Rev John and John William as shareholders, each liable for an equal share of any profits, debts and in raising capital to continue working the mine. It was a partnership that was to lead to disaster and the total estrangement, within eight years, of John William and his father.

19th July

My Father & I attended the Sherrifs Court the miners had brought an action against My Father for not paying them They swore it was by day wage when it was by bargain We returned home

20th July

My Father RD & I went fishing in the lake above Havedtany (sic) Craig

Beddgelert.

21st July

My Father & 7 others went to Beddgelert Church My Father & I called on Mr Hutton.

22nd July

My Father RD.DH. & I went to Snodon Mr Ellis called.

23rd July

My Father and RD went to Snodon I went to Innamaddock [?] to tender the ballance of a bill to the well wright but he was not at home I told his daughter if he would take a stamped receipt to Mr Kent he would pay him The Tattons took tea here.

On August 6th the Rev John went to Froghall wharf to meet his shipment of copper ore which John William had seen weighed and sampled. He records that it weighed 34 tons and 9cwts. A similar amount of ore which had arrived at Whiston Copper works in 1831 had been worth £8 0s 0d (£450). Carriage of the ore from Froghall up to Whiston was expensive, as the following entry shows, and to overcome this, the Sneyds embarked on an ambitious scheme for an aerial rail track worked on an hydraulic principal. Although started it was never completed though signs of it are still just visible in the fields.

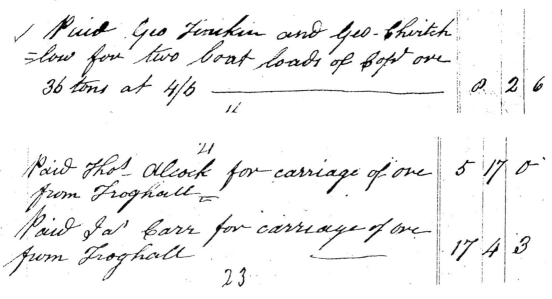

Extracts from the original Whiston account books. 1831-43

Courtesy of Lindsey Porter

Ore being transferred from the barges at Froghall, mid to late 19th century.

The ore that John William had seen onto the ship was then taken up to Liverpool, passing two smelters, one at at Holyhead and the other at Liverpool. From there it was transferred onto barges and made its way through the Trent and Mersey canal system to Froghall Wharf in Staffordshire, where it was met by the Rev John. He recorded in his diary of 1844,

Tuesday Aug. 6th I walked to Froghall to see two boat loads of copper ore weighed and sampled. It weighed 34 tons and 9 cwts.

The samples of ore taken at Caernarvon were very important, for otherwise the ore could have been made even less valuable by the substitution of rock for ore somewhere along the journey. As it was, it was not a very high yielding ore. The best they could have hoped for was probably about 7% of copper per ton of ore, and frequently it was less than this. The Sneyds owned the copper smelting works at Whiston and the ore was taken up there from Froghall Wharf. The copper yielded from this load would have been about 2 tons 4 cwts and worth about £7-8 per ton. (£800)

24th July

My Father RD DH left in the poney cariage for home I went to Caernarvon to see the copper weighed sampled and shopped [shipped]

25th July

I went to Snodon I heard WB had not come home till 10 o'clock in the morning that he only took 1..16..4 in an average day & that he did not bring vouchers for the corn he bought I blew him up & told him he must come home in better time take 2 tons and bring vouchers for everything.

26th July
I went to the mine

27th July
I stayed at home and took a Hollyday (sic)

28th July
H. PM. & I walkd to church at Beddgelert in the afternoon it rained

29th July
I went to the mine It rained all day William Brunt did not go to Carenarvon because my Grandfathers horse had lost a shoe

30th July
I rode to the mine It was a very wet day there was not any copper carted from the engine house

31st July *I stayed at home it rained all day*

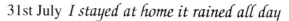

August

1st August

I stayed at home It rained all day

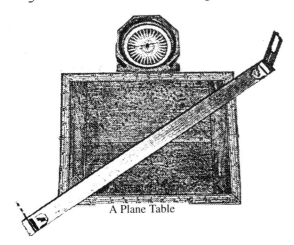

A Plane Table

2nd August

I rode to the mine Mr David Davies and I dialed the level the top of John Owens level It rained a little

To dial a level - a surveying term meaning to measure the length and direction of the level or tunnel. It was done with a plane table and a compass.

3rd August

I rode my horse to Caernarvon to enquire of Ellis Jones about some bills & paid him them It was very wet

4th August

We walked to Beddgelert Church in the afternoon

St Mary's Church, Beddgelert

The church had its origins in a Celtic Christian community established on the present site in the 6th century. It is said to be the oldest religious foundation in Wales. Beddgelert was about three and a half miles from Plas Gwynant, along the same road that is today, the A498. The family walked to church almost every Sunday. It had to be exceptionally wet to prevent them from attending. Even when the Rev John was at home in Staffordshire, the children still went to the church.

5th August

It rained all day and I stayed at home

6th August

It rained all day I went as far as the cottages in the afternoon The two cart horses and man that brings the ore from the Engion (sic) house were blown off the road

Plas Gwynant is now owned by Sandwell Borough Council and is used as an outward bound centre.

7th August

I left Plas Gwynnant at $^{1}/_{2}$ past 8 to met the mail to Caernarvon at Beddgelert & got on by the Chester Mail to Chester I walked round the walls and looked about the town & slept at the Feathers Inn

Chester.

Chester

8th August

I walked round the walls went into court & looked about the town I went to the station in an Omnibus & from thence to Whitmore by railway from thence to Shelton by omnibus I walked home from there I had some lunch at Rownall on my way

Whitmore is on the A53 Newcastle to Market Drayton road. Shelton is in Stoke-on-Trent. The walk home was a distance of about seven miles. The court room was in the Shire Hall, and sounds very similar to the one in Stafford, where his father was a magistrate. It was described at the time as being *"a spacious, semi-circular hall, lighted from above. The county prison is behind, on a lower level, whence the prisoners are brought into the dock by a flight of steps. In a higher ward there is an armoury, where from 30 to 40 thousand stands of arms, and other munitions of war, are constantly kept".*

A Guide Book to Wales, 1851

Watergate Street, Chester

Eastgate Street, Chester

Eastgate Street, Chester.

Bridge Street, Chester

Bridge Street, Chester.

9th August
My Father & I stayed about home and looked at the building

10th August
I rode the Mare to the Paddock to ask David Keeling if he could bring the piece of wood he found under the ground here without cutting it

11th August
My Father & I went to Ipstones in the morning and Foxt in the afternoon

12th August
My Father Mr Bradshaw Mr Clewes of Westenshire [?] Uncle Tom met at Mixon Hay to shoot The first two named did not shoot We killed 8 brace 3 hares & a snipe

13th August
I rode up to the moors Uncle & Aunt Tom came up in the afternoon We killed 4 brace & 3 snipe & a cat My Father walked to the Paddock

14th August
My Father & I went to Leek called on Mr Heathcote and left Mr Heathcote a brace of Grouse We also called on Mr Barnes Mr Brindley and Mr Edwin Heaton

Waterhouses is a village in the Staffordshire Moorlands. Sarah Wettenhall, an ancestor of the Ashcombe Sneyds, had been the daughter and heiress of Edward Wettenhall of Waterhouses.

15th August
My Father & I went up to the moors It was the fair at Blackwear and was very well attended We had tea at Mr Bakers of the Waterhouse Mrs Helman left We killed 2 brace

16th August   *Mrs Brindley called*

17th August
My Father & I went to Whiston called on Shaw & on Mr Brandon of Cheadle Whiston brought 1 grouse and 1 brown hen down from the moors

18th August
My Father & I went to Ipstones in the Morning and Foxt in the afternoon

19th August

My Father & I went to Bradnop to examine the papers in the village chest Called to see Thompson of Blake Lee who is very ill

The Rev John was Lord of the Manor of Bradnop. These papers included deeds to many local properties dating back to the 16th century. Many of them survive, annotated in Rev John's handwriting, in Keele University Library.

Alton Towers c1890
One of John William's cousins, Mary Jane Sneyd Kynnersley, "Minnie", married Dr Fraser, vicar of Alton. The Sneyds often visited Alton, and from time to time went to Alton Towers, home of the Shrewsburys.

20th August

My Father dined and slept at Farley I dined at Alton and met H.R.H. the Duke of Cambridge & the Douchis (sic)   Farley was the seat of the Bill family.

21st August

My Father left Mr Bills and I Alton Towers in the Faitent (sic) after Breakfast We attended the Justice meeting in Leek

22nd August

My Father & I stayed at home all day Mr Challenor called and he dined with us

23rd August

My Father & I stayed about home all morning We called at Ashcombe & Witley Abbey

24th August

Uncle & I went up to the moors I calld on Robert Baker & took him with us We killed 1 grouse 3 snipes 1 hare I killed everything

25th August

My Father & I went to Ipstones in the morning & Foxt in the afternoon

26th August

My Father Mother EJ. DH. & I with them on horse left Basford for Plas Gwynnant and travailed as far as Whitchurch.

27th August

We travailed from Whitchurch and saw the kenels (sic) at Whinstay My Father & I walked to the British Iron Works at Ruabon

The Iron Works, Coalbrookdale. By 1844 the industrialisation of Britain was well advanced and the Sneyds were taking advantage of the new forms of transport - railway, steamer, etc. The Rev John also took his children to see modern industrial sites and they all visited the huge British Iron Works at Ruabon on their journey to or from Wales. The development of the iron industry was central to the whole progress of trade and prosperity in the country and the huge foundries which spewed their sulphurous fumes and sparks into the night sky were considered a major tourist attraction.   *Aquatint in the Mansell collection*

Lithograph of Nant Gwynant.
This view would also have been familiar to John William. Plas Gwynant, the house the Sneyds rented, was close by.

28th August
We travailed from Corwen & found all quite well at Plas Gwynnant

29th August
My Father & I rode to the mine & inspected it My Father rode Meakin & I on my Horse

Forge

Foundry

30th August

My Father & all excepting GA in all 11 of us
went in the boat on Lynn Gwynnant My Father
H. EJ. PM. S. & I walked to the top of Snodon &
and saw the sun set & stayed out all night

Local legend requires every one who lives near to Snowdon to
spend at least one night on the summit. According to the
Ancient Britons, whoever sleeps upon the summit will
awaken inspired.

From *A Book for Boys and Girls*, 1861

From Columbia Lady's and Gentleman's Magazine,
May 1847

31st August

My Father H. EJ. PM. S. & I saw the
sun rise from the top of Snodon Sisters
returned home by themselves My Father
& I by the mines

Unbelievably, John William's sisters would have
been dressed something like this for their climb up
Mount Snowdon. They would have worn stout
lace-up boots, their skirts would probably have
been looped up to expose their ankles, and their
bonnets would have been less highly trimmed, but
convention demanded that their clothes would
have conformed to this style and been worn over
corsets and layers of voluminous cotton under
garments. Thirteen year old Susanna might have
been allowed a shorter, calf-length skirt, but the
other girls were young women and would have
had to dress accordingly. Harriet was twenty,
Emily nineteen and Penelope Marianne eighteen.

Illustration of copper mining in Wales by Malcolm Newton,
Reproduced by courtesy of the Sygon Copper Mine Museum, Beddgelert.

September

1st September
Fourteen of us went to Beddgelert Church

2nd September
Mr & Mrs Pascoe came here to breakfast Mr P went with my Father & me to our mine

3rd September
My Father H. EJ. S. & I went to see the Bulchley mine

4th September
My Father & I rod (sic) to Pen-y-pass We went as far as the top of the sledge road

Illustration of Welsh miners by Malcolm Newton,
Reproduced by courtesy of the Sygon Copper Mine Museum, Beddgelert.

5th September

My Father & I rode to Mr Kents We paid the miners £286. 5. 10 We rode as far as Pen-y-[?]

6th September

I took the Phaitent up to Pen -y- Pass My Father Mother EJ. L. M. F. & I went as far as the engion (sic) house My Father & I went to the mine

7th September

My Father & I walked to view the Llewed mines We got very wet My Uncle Kynnesley died

8th September

My Father Mother EJ.H.PM.S.L.F.& I went to Beddgelert Church

9th September

My Father & I rode to the mine my Father on Meakin I on My horse to view the mine.

10th September

My Father Mother H.EJ.P.S.M. F. went to Caernarvon in the Phaitent My Father went on the coach to see Mr Williams of Beaumaris I drove home .

11th September

I rode to the Buckley mine to measure the Railway Wagons and examine other things My Father returned from Bangor.

Railway wagons carrying ore.

12th September

My Father & I walked to the Bulckley Mine we made an arraingment (sic) with Mr Pascoe to visit the Snodon Mine 4 days a month for £3 per month or 30£ a year Mr Hutton & Mr Brewer dined here.

13th September

My Father Mr Pascoe & I went to Pen y Pass in the Phaitent on the way to the mine We examined all the levils (sic) Mr P breakfasted here This is the first day of his attending as Captain of our mine

Whiston Copper Works

Mr Pascoe was appointed to be mine manager by the Sneyds on 12th September. He lived in Beddgelert with his wife and the church register records the birth of a daughter, Ellen born to William and Ellen Pascoe 25th April 1840, and a son Francis James born in July 1842. The Sneyds had known Mr Pascoe for some years having had dealings with him whilst buying ore for the Whiston Copper Works. He was an obvious choice as manager of their mine and a friendly working relationship was set up. Mrs Sneyd and her husband visited their home and took tea with Mrs Pascoe.

Access to the mine was difficult as, until a causeway was built in 1853, all the ore had to be taken across the lake on boats, then transferred to wagons to be taken by road to Caernarvon where it was weighed and shipped.

14th September
My Father & I stayed at home it was very wet Mr Ellis called.

15th September
A very wet day we stayed at home.

16th September
My Father & I walked to Llanwyd Mr Brewers and the Bulchley Mines

17th September
My Father & I rode to the mine.

18th September
My Father & I rode to Snodon

19th September
My Father Mother H. EJ. PM. S. & I went in the Pheaton (sic) to Pen-y-Pass and from thence walked to the top of Snodon accompanied by two frenchmen.

20th September
My Father and a large party of us went in the pheaton (sic) to call on Mrs Jackson with whom we lunched My Father bought 2 tons of hay from him for 9.0.0. We Called on Mr Ellis

Fashion plate from *Le Moniteur de la Mode,* Summer 1844, showing dress for country wear. John William's mother and younger brothers and sisters probably dressed very much like this whilst on holiday in Wales.

21st September

My Father & I rode to the mine The Females went to the Fare (sic) at Beddgelert.

22nd September

My Father & a large party of us went to Beddgelert Church in the afternoon

23rd September

Mr Pascoe breakfasted here My Father Mr Pascoe & I went to the mine in the Phaitent Mr Pascoe set the making of 2 slime pits for £1.5s each at the bottom of the haries [?]

The slime pits were a reservoir in which the metallic slimes were collected that had been washed out of spoil in the form of a slurry. They were rich in mineral ore.

Snowdon and Llanberis Lakes

24th September

I drove my Father in the Phaitent to meet the coach at Beddgelert He went home and went to call on Mr Pears at Ruthin on his way I went to see the Bulchley Mine & took my Gun on my way to Penegwyrig but only killed a Water Hen

25th September
I went to the mine.

26th September
I went to the Mine

27th September
My Mother H. EJ. PM. S.JC. & I went in the Phaitent to Penn-y-Pass I went to the Mine the others walked to Llanberis

28th September
I stayed at home rote (sic) to my Father and went out shooting in the afternoon but found nothing

29th September
A large party of us went to Beddgelert Church to hear the Welsh Service Mr Marsden preached Mr Ellis was from home and there was no English Service

30th September
I rode my Horse to Caernarvon called at Penn-y-Pass paid John Owen for Hay £8 10s

Basket of fruit - drawing from Ralph De Tunstall's scrapbook.
Reproduced courtesy of Keele University Library

October

1st October

When Mr Pascoe & I got to the Mine there was not a single person there so we made up gun miners to sign 5 of them 2s 6d and Davis 1s Mr Pascoe & I rode to the mine together Mr Pascoe stoped (sic) the men sleeping in the bottom levil (sic) & set them a bargain to clean the sump in the second levil for 5d to put the m--[?] up and 5d a fathom to clean the sump

Gun miners: those miners who placed the plugs of gun powder into the rock face - a very dangerous job.

2nd October

I rode to the mine on my Horse it rained and was very windy

3rd October

I stayed at home a wet day

4th October

I drove my Mother H. EJ. P. & M. in the Phaitent to Benegured [?] I went on to Llanberris to meet the wagon bringing some slate for the Engin (sic) house 600 in number The remainder of the party walked to Capel Curig

Capel Curig

A Guide Book to Wales, published in 1851, describes the pass of Llanberis through which John William would have gone as, '*a scene of wild grandeur and fearful sublimity of the most impressive and majestic character,*'

5th October
I stayed at home a wet day

6th October
My Mother H. EJ.PM.S.L.M.F. & I went to Beddgelert Church in the afternoon

7th October
I went to the Mine

8th October
Mr Pascoe & I went to the Mine

9th October
My Birthday a very wet day I stayed at home

10th October
Mr Pascoe & I went to the Mine I went very early We measured all the work and set the bargains It is the setting day

11th October
I drove my Mother H. EJ. P. S. EL.M.F. to Tremadock We walked to Port Maddock from thence I paid a bill for corn 18s

Tremadoc

Tremadoc was named after W. Alexander Maddock who had successfully regained a tract of marshy land from the sea and turned it into rich arable farm land in 1800. It was a fashionable place to visit and boasted a fine market house and assembly room. The road from Beddgelert to Tremadoc and Portmadoc, some one mile further on from where copper and slate was exported, was well known for the grandeur of the scenery through which it passed. It is essentially the same road today.

12th October

I stayed at home & went out shooting and killed a hearon (sic) ect.ect.ect. PM Capel Curig

13th October

My Mother H.EJ.P.& I went in the Phaitent to Beddlegert Church in the afternoon

14th October

I stayed at home with a bad cold A wet day

15th October

My Father came from out of Staffordshire I drove the Phaitent to Beddgelert to meet him

16th October

My Father Mr Pascoe & I went up to the Mine in the Phaitent

17th October

My Father and I attended to the Mining accounts at home .

18th October

My Father & I attended to the mining accounts at home and went out fishing.

19th October

My Father & I went up to the cottage on Snodon and paid the workmen

20th October

I left this place for Home on my Horse to meet the Leek Volanteers to have a dinner and drill at Leek on Thursday I rode as far as Corwen where I stayd the night

21st October

I rode from Corwen to Whitchurch where I slept My Father H. PM. EL.JC. left Plas Gwynnant for home they travailed (sic) by coach.

22nd October
I rode from Whitchurch to Basford My Father H. PM. EL. JC. reached home

23rd October
My Father attended the Justice meeting at Leek I went out shooting with Whiston and killed 3 rabbits

24th October
I rode my Horse to a drill in Birchy Dale field I had the command I attended a troop dinner at the Red Lion Mr Child was in the chair there were about 60 of the troop & a good many Gentlemen & Farmers My Father was there but neither Mr Ackers or Mr Crann It passed off very well

Leek Market place showing the Red Lion Hotel, from an illustration by W R Kean

25th October
I went out shooting with Whiston & killed 1 hare 1 pheasant & 9 rabbits My Father stayed about home

26th October
My Father & I went to Whiston in the gig with the young black horse We had some lunch at Mr Keys

Crakemarsh was the home of Sir Thomas and Lady Shepherd and is near Uttoxeter. The house was built c1820, but around the remains of earlier buildings. John William's grandfather, William Sneyd, was a great friend of the Shepherds. The rest of the family also visited them, and John William would have known Crakemarsh well. The house is now derelict.

27th October

My Father & I went as far as Ipstones in the gig & walked on to Foxt in the morning & came back to Ipstones in the afternoon

28th October

My Father & I rode to Rownall to breakfast My Father went with Mr Childs in his carriage & I on my horse to attend an agricultural meeting at Newcastle Lane Sandon was in the chair & Mr Sneyd of Keele was appointed president & Lord Tabbit vice president for the ensuing year My Father & I dined & drank tea at Ashcombe My Grandfather had a letter from Sir Thomas Shepperd containing the intelligence that Uncle Tom when shooting at Crakemarsh had while loading his gun he supposed through a spark in the barrel burst his powder flask and injured both hands very much

29th October

I went out shooting with Whiston and killed 1 hare 3 partridges & 12 rabbits My Father stayed at home settling Mr Bakers accounts

Advertisement for Churnet Valley Railway shares. *North Staffordshire Mercury*, Saturday, June 15th, 1844.

30th

My Father & I attended a Justice meeting in Leek & called at Ashcombe & drove as far as Newcastle in the gig We went onto Whichurch in the Omnibus & from thence to Chester by rails and from thence to Caernarvon per Mail in the night.

31st

My Father & I called on Mr Powel the lawyer at Caernarvon about the action a miner is bringing agaist my Father on Tuesday next We went to Beddgelert per Mail and walked to Plas Gwynnant

Railway travel was in its infancy in 1844, when the Rev John and John William travelled from Whitchurch to Chester "by rails", but this was soon to change. The Sneyds were much involved with the Churnet Valley Railway This opened in July 1849. John William's father, Rev John Sneyd, was present with "*several of the principal gentlemen in the neighbourhood*" when the first bricks were laid in the tunnel near Leek in November 1847 and the contractor, Mr Tredwell, provided champagne at the site, followed by a dinner at the Red Lion in Leek. *Staffordshire Advertiser* 20th November 1847. Many members of the family had shares in the Churnet Valley line and other railways in Britain and later abroad. It was part of a pattern of investment. In the 18th and early 19th centuries, John William's grandfather, William Sneyd, had been a shareholder in the Trent and Mersey Canal, and both he and Rev John were involved with various local turnpike trusts.

All the Sneyd diaries record a great deal of travel by rail. The coming of the railways had a major impact on their visiting patterns. It became possible for them to travel greater distances within the day and, whereas in the early 19th century diaries, dinner guests usually stayed the night, it became increasingly possible for guests to return home after an evening out.

November

1st November
My Father Mr Taylor Mr Pascoe & I went up to Snowden (sic) in a car to view the Mine

2nd November
My Father & I met Mr Taylor & Mr Pascoe at the Bulchley Mine

John Taylor in 1825.
From a portrait by Sir Thomas Lawrence for the Athenaeum Club.

John Taylor (1779-1863) was one of the most respected mining authorities of his age. Born in Norwich he had taken over one of Devonshire's largest copper mines when he was only nineteen and made a resounding success of it. He was involved with the Geological Society of London and more than anyone else transformed the traditional practices of British mining into a scientific discipline. That the Sneyds called on his expertise is perhaps an indication of their worries about the Snowdon mine and the other mine in which they had interests, the Llwydd Mine. His advice came too late. On 14th November the results of his investigations were given to the Rev John. Perhaps he had been expecting bad news for he took two of his daughters with him for company.

3rd November
My Father EJ. S. & I walked to Beddgelert Church in the afternoon we called on Mr Pascoe & Mr Marsden.

4th November
My Father rode Meakin to Caernarvon to try to get the trial altered but Mr Powell had made an agreement with Lloyd Roberts EJ. S. & I walked to Dolwyndellon Castle 15 miles away

5th November
My Father & Mr Pascoe rode to the mine they measured the length between the levils (sic) I stayed at home for I had a sore heel It was very wet .

6th November
My Father & I stayed at home My Father read a good deal of The Last of the Moiakins [Mohicans]to us

7th November
My Father EJ.S. & I walked to Cumdilly Fall and to Glentire and then copeid the last two months accounts into my Fathers books

8th November
My Father & I walked to the Llewyn mine to the Snodon Mine where we met Mr Pascoe It was the survey day

9th November
My Father & I stayed at home

10th November
My Father EJ. S. & I walked to Beddgelert Church in the afternoon My Father promised Mr Ellis to preach next Sunday.

11th November
I left Plas Gwynnant & reached home at about three in the morning My Father went to Bangor to se Mr Williams etc

12th November
I call'd at Belmont for the first time since Uncle Toms accident .

13th November *I called at Belmont.*

14th November
Whiston & I went to Belmont & killed 3 couple of rabbits & 1 hare.

15th November
Whiston & I went out shooting we killed 15 rabbits 3 hares & 1 pheasant I dined at Ashcombe

16th November
Whiston & I went out shooting & killed 2 brace of Partridge

17th November
I took the Gig to Ipstones in the morning and walked with Uncle John to Fox[t]

18th November
Whiston & I went out shooting 1 brace partridges 1 snipe & 7 rabbits

19th November
Harriet & I rode to call at Woodlands H. on Cathlene I on my Horse

20th November
Whiston & I went out shooting we went to Mr Johnsons & Mr Bills woods & killed 1 woodcock 1 pheasant & 5 rabbits I took the Gig to Newcastle to meet my Father on his way out of Wales He arrived at Newcastle at 12 o'clock at night

Woodcock

21st November

My Father & I walked over to Ashcombe & called on my Grandfather & Uncle Henry We walkd to call on Uncle Tom at Belmont & went in the gig to dine at Ashcombe

22nd November

My Father & I went to Cheadle in the Gig We called on Mr Inglby about selling the Whiston Copper, on Catlow about the 4 Waits viz Owen John William Henry & another at Ashcombe & called on Mr Marsden about the 4 Waits

The Waits were church singers who performed at Christmas time.

23rd November

Uncle & Aunt Tom called My Father & I met the Bishop at dinner at Mr Heathcotes

24th November

My Father H. P. attended the 3 services at Leek Church & heard the Bishop preach twice & dined at Mr Barnes My Father went to Ipstones & Foxt and heard the Bishop preach at Leek in the evening

A drawing by the Rev John at the age of fourteen.

102

Wetley Rocks, near Cheddleton. The dramatic rocks behind the village were much admired by travellers.

25th November

My Father Uncle Henry & I went to Wetley Rocks to meet the Bishop he look'd over the Church and examined the school chldren My Father & I called at Fox Earth My Father H. & I dined & stayed the night at Cliffe Ville

St John's Church, Wetley Rocks, was built in 1833-4 and endowed by Jane Debank, John William's grandmother. His Uncle Henry, his father's youngest brother, was "perpetual curate" there.

Schools were still tied to the Church of England at this time and the quality varied enormously from parish to parish, depending on the enthusiasm of the local vicar and the committment of the Bishop. The Rev John cared about education and was involved in the local schools. He took his own children on educational trips, loved books and was a fine artist. John William does not seem to have inherited these particular interests or skills, but his son did.
Picture from *Illustrated London News*. 1852

26th November

My Father H. & I returned from Cliff Ville & called at Weston Coyning I went as far as Sandon in the Gig on my way to the Litchfield Ball & from thence in Mr Tomlinsons carriage there were about 150 persons preasant (sic) My Father walkd to Ashcombe

Dinner was an important ritual in the 19th century. This illustration, from a mid 19th century short story, shows a table set for dessert with an elaborate centrepiece of fruit and flowers. It appars in one of the scrapbooks kept by John William's son Ralph De Tunstall Sneyd in the late 1860s. *Courtesy of Keele University Library*

27th November

I returned with Mr Tomlinsn in his carriage as far as Sandon & thence in the Gig My Father walked to Leek .... (entry erased)

28th November

My Father Mother PM. & I dined at Woodlands .... (entry erased)

29th November

My Father Mother H. & I dined at Ash Hall My Father & I went to Cheadle in the Gig and called on Mr Catlow & Mr Brandon

30th November

Sergeant Major Dean Whiston & I went shooting in Mr Johnsons wood & killd 2 pheasant 1 partridge 1 snipe 1 woodcock 4 rabbits My Father Mother PM. & I dined at Belmont We met Mr & Mrs Dunbar & Uncle John

December

1st December

My Father Mother H. PM. L. & I went to Ipstones Church in the morning My Father & Uncle John went to Foxt

2nd December

Gustavus was Christened by Uncle Henry at Wetley Rocks Church Mr & Mrs Hassells & Mr Bradshaw & Uncle John dined & stayed the night Mr & Mrs Barnes Uncle & Aunt Henry Mr & Mrs & Miss Foudrinier dined here

3rd December

Mr Bradshaw & Mr & Mrs Hassells left & Uncle John after lunch Uncle & Aunt Tom Mrs Dunbar & Aunt Mary called

4th December

My Father & I attended the Justice meeting at Leek Mr Bullock was brought up for buying game off a poacher I Joined my Father in signing a noat (sic) of hand lent by Mr Sleigh of Leek £1000

5th December

Whiston & I went shooting in Mr Johnsons wood we killed 1 brace of pheasants 1 partridge 1 hare & 7 rabbits

6th December

I went out shooting & killd 1 partridge My Father stayd at home making an act concerning churches My Father Mother H. & I dined at Ashcombe

7th December

My Father went to Ashcombe & from thence with Aunt Mary to Loxley where he stayed the night to see Cousin Tom about the Loxley estate Mr Daley [?]called

Loxley Park is near Uttoxeter. It looks late Georgian but the staircase and some of the interior is apparently late 17th century. It was the home of the Kynnersleys. John William's great grandfather, John Sneyd, married Penelope Kynnersley, co-heir with her brother Clement to the Loxley estate. The estate was inherited by John William's grandfather's younger brother, Thomas, (1774-1844), who took the surname Sneyd-Kynnersley. On Thomas's death there was obviously some question over the future of the estate. The house survives and is now a boy's boarding school.

8th December

My Father took both duties at Dilhorn I stayed at home with a cold My Father returned home from Loxley

9th December

My Father walked to Ashcombe I went out rabbiting with Gip & killed 8 rabbits

10th December

My Father went to Stone on his way to Stafford to the assizes on his way to Wales I went out rabbiting with Gip & killed 26 rabbits & 3 hares I Killed 12 rabbits & 1 Hare

11th December

Whiston & I went out shooting we killed 8 rabbits

12th December

Whiston & I went out shooting We killed 1 hare 1 snipe & 3 rabbits My Mother Uncle John H. & I dined at Mr Barnes

13th December

I stayed at home making a plan of the old house

14th December

Whiston & I went out shooting 1 woodcock 1hare I snipe & 3 rabbits Ralph Dean & Driden (sic) came home from Ashbourne

15th December

Ralph Dean H.DH.L. & I went to Ipstones in the morning My Father went to church at Beddgelert

16th December

Whiston & I went out shooting We killed 1woodcock 1brace of pratridge 1 snipe & 3 rabbits and a wild duck Ralph Dean rode to Mr Bafners.

Wrappers from Curtis and Harvey's Gunpowder. John William's great passion, all his life, seems to have been shooting. This is apparent both from his own 1844 diary, and also from the diaries [1858-1889] of his sister Susanna, who lived with him as his housekeeper after he was widowed in June 1862. She brought up his only son Ralph De Tunstall Sneyd, born May 1862. The scrapbooks she and Ralph De Tunstall made when he was a small child survive and many of these gunpowder wrappers, printed in bright red and blue, are pasted into them.

Reproduced by courtesy of Keele University Library

17th December
Whiston Dean & I went out shooting Whiston & I killed 1 pheasant 1 hare & 8 rabbits

18th December
I rode my horse to Mr Mycocks of Waterfall to get the lock of my gun mended.

19th December
I stayed about home.

20th December
I Rode to Mr Mycocks of Waterfall to fetch the lock of my gun which he had been mending.

21st December
My Father EJ. S. M. & Ileen arriving from Plas Gwynnant Whiston & I went out shooting & killd 1 woodcock etc

22nd December
My Father preached at Foxt and Uncle at Ipstones

23rd December
My Father & RD. walked to Ashcombe Two carts loaded with goods arrived from Plas Gwynnant I went to look for wild ducks

24th December
We kept Christmas eve My Father walked to Ashcombe

Snapdragon was a game, usually played at Christmas, in which raisins were snatched from a bowl of flaming brandy or other spirit, and eaten whilst still alight.

25th December
My Father preached at Ipstones and Uncle at Foxt We had some games snapdragon etc

26th December
My Father & I attended the justice meeting at Leek & gave Mr Cruso a recipt for £5 on the death Richard Gaunt of Leek

27th December
My Father & I went to Cheadle on Mr Kentons bussiness on the Borde (sic) of Guardians

28th December
Aunt Mary & her Children dined here

29th December
My Father & RD. went to Foxt in the morning H. EJ. D, L. & I went to Ipstones in the afternoon

30th December

My Father RD. & I went to Mr Fords of Cliffords Wood where we left RD. to se if he liked farming We looked over Swinerton Hall and my Father & I went on to Stafford

As John William was to inherit the estate, professions had to be found for the younger sons. Ralph Debank was only fourteen but his father was already looking to his future. Ralph died young, but two of his brothers went abroad to farm. Lionel was sent to a ranch in America, which he hated, and sent letters home begging to be allowed to return. At last his father relented and sent him £20 for the return journey, but it was too late. Lionel was already ill, and he died of fever off New Orleans, aboard the ship that was bringing him home. He was just nineteen. Dryden Henry went to New Zealand in 1852 and farmed at Kaiapoi for fourteen years before returning home.

31st December1

My Father & I went in the court and dined at Mr Salts and slept there .

Church of St Edward, Cheddleton

In 1844 the Sneyds usually attended church at Ipstones because Rev John did duty there. Cheddleton church was actually nearer and sometimes the women of the family went there rather than making the long uphill journey to Ipstones. After the Rev John's resignation in 1861, the family became much more involved with Cheddleton church.

John William, Susanna Ingleby and his son, Ralph De Tunstall. John William is wearing his Yeomanry uniform. Susanna (1831-91) was John William's sister and was his housekeeper from 1862 until her death.

Photograph by W J Lapworth, Stafford, August 21st 1868

John William Sneyd
Photograph by Elliott & Fry. 55 Baker Street, London.

June 4th 1873

Sources

The sources of many of the illustrations are indicated in the text. a number of oil paintings, watercolours, photographs, prints and postcards are in private collections. In addition, the authors wish to acknowledge the following sources:

History of the Ancient Parish of Leek. John Sleigh 1883.
Olde Leeke. M.H.Miller 1891.
Picturesque Views of Staffordshire. William West with engravings by
Frederick Calvert, 1830.
Illustrations of the Natural Scenery of the Snowdonian Mountains. H.L.Jones, 1829.
Richard Doyle's Diary, c 1840.
Ralph de Tunstall Sneyd's Scrapbook.
Chambers' Book of Days.
A Guide Book to Wales. 1851
The Horseman. R.H.Hershberger, 1844
John Taylor. R.Burt.
The Country Year Book. T.Miller. Chapman 1847.
Beautiful Britain. Werner 1894.
Illustrated London News
North Staffordshire Mercury.
Columbia Lady's and Gentleman's Magazine. May 1847.
Le Moniteur de la Mode. Summer 1844.
Punch, 1851.
Etchings by Mackarness, c1890.
R. and W. Wright. Stafford 1859.
Staffordshire Views. W.L.Walters.
William Salt Library, Stafford.
Staffordshire Museum Service.
Keele University Collection.
National Newspaper Library.
Staffordshire Yeomanry Collection.
Mansell Collection.
Borough Museum, Newcastle under Lyme.
Sygon Copper Mine Museum, Beddgelert.

Sneyd
Nec Opprimre Nec Opprimi